IN PRAISE OF EDWARD DE BONO

'Edward doesn't just think. He is a one-man global industry, whose work is gospel in government, universities, schools, corporates and even prisons all over the world' *Times 2*

'Edward de Bono is a toolmaker, his tools have been fashioned for thinking, to make more of the mind' Peter Gabriel

'De Bono's work may be the best thing going in the world today' George Gallup, originator of the Gallup Poll

'The guru of clear thinking' *Marketing Week*

PRAISE FOR *HOW TO HAVE A BEAUTIFUL MIND*

'Mercifully free of the trite techniques offered by many publications promising to save us from social awkwardness, the book succeeds in doing just that' *Independent on Sunday*

'a clever, instructive guide . . . Highly recommended' *The Good Book Guide*

PRAISE FOR *HOW TO HAVE CREATIVE IDEAS*

'Good fun, stimulating good thinking' *Times Educational Supplement*

'A thought-provoking – and thought-improving – book . . . Simple, practical and great fun' *Management Today*

'It is simple, practical and fun and a necessary read for anyone who wants to have great ideas' *Business Executive*

Think!

Before It's Too Late

Edward de Bono

Vermilion
LONDON

1 3 5 7 9 10 8 6 4 2

Published in 2009 by Vermilion, an imprint of Ebury Publishing

Ebury Publishing is a Random House Group company

Copyright © The McQuaig Group Inc. 2009

Edward de Bono has asserted his moral right to be identified as the author of this Work in accordance with the Copyright, Design and Patents Act 1988.

The Random House Group Limited Reg. No. 954009

Addresses for companies within the Random House Group can be found at www.rbooks.co.uk

A CIP catalogue record for this book is available from the British Library

Printed and bound in Australia by
Griffin Press

ISBN 9780091924096

Copies are available at special rates for bulk orders. Contact the sales development team on 020 7840 8487 for more information.

To buy books by your favourite authors and register for offers, visit www.rbooks.co.uk

CONTENTS

Author's Note

Apologies

There are a number of people whose names should be in this book. They have told me certain things, or done certain things, and I would like to acknowledge their contribution. Unfortunately I do not keep detailed records of all meetings and conversations. So I apologise to anyone who feels they should have been mentioned. Please write to me and indicate where and why your name should be included, and in the next edition of the book I shall see that your name is there.

In addition, if you have practical experience with my thinking in your own life or business, or in teaching the methods, and it is not included here, let me have details and, if appropriate, I will include them in the next edition.

Any omission of a name is unintentional and I apologise for it. I do want to give full credit to those who have helped me in my work.

Introduction

WHY DO WE NEED THIS BOOK?

This is not a nice book. It is not intended to be a nice book. You cannot shift complacency with niceness. We are completely complacent about the quality of our human thinking. We believe it to be wonderful for various reasons that I shall discuss later. We have done nothing about human thinking, outside of mathematics, for roughly 2,400 years, since the great Greek philosophers. I do not believe we should be so complacent. This book is about why human thinking is so poor. It also suggests what we can do about it. So it is a positive book even if the need for such a book is negative.

I come from the island of Malta, which is officially the oldest civilisation in the world. The earliest man-made structure on earth is a substantial Stone Age temple in Gozo (the sister island of Malta). So perhaps I have a mission to save the world from its complacency.

Think grey not green

It has become very fashionable to 'think green', and I am fully in favour of this. Climate change is a legitimate political theme, and any politician can express his or her concern with this matter and get votes as a result. This is excellent.

But there is a bigger and more urgent danger than climate change. That danger is the poor quality of human thinking. This requires even more urgent attention. Perhaps there should be an even more important slogan 'think grey'. The grey refers to our grey matter, or brains. Most of the problems, conflicts and fights in the world are caused by poor thinking. An improvement in human thinking would help solve such issues. If we get our thinking right then it becomes easier to solve not only environmental problems, but other problems too.

Consider the Israel / Palestine problem. Here we have some of the most intelligent people on the surface of the earth. For over 60 years they have been unable to solve their problem, and yet they know full well that it has to be solved some time. That is poor thinking.

Nothing is more fundamental or more important than human thinking. What about values? The purpose of thinking is to enable us to deliver and enjoy our values. Values without thinking are highly dangerous and have been responsible for the wars, pogroms, persecutions and appalling behaviour of the past. Thinking without values is pointless – for thinking then has no purpose.

Yet, amazingly, we have paid no attention to thinking for 2,400 years.

Emotion vs. thought

What about emotions? What about human behaviour? What about human nature?

There is a belief that thinking is academic and abstract and that what really drives action is human emotions and human behaviour. This is unfortunate nonsense that arises directly – and correctly – from our traditional methods of thinking, which have very little practical impact in conflict situations.

In the Karee platinum mine in South Africa there were seven tribes represented among the workers: Xhosa, Zulu, Sutu, and so on. As a consequence of the traditional hostilities between these tribes, developed over centuries, there were 210 fights every month between members of the various tribes. Susan Mackie and Donalda Dawson taught my perceptual thinking to these totally illiterate miners who had never been to school for even one day in their lives. They encouraged them to consider other people's points of view. The result was that the fights dropped from 210 a month to just four! Why had better thinking made this huge difference? Because this new thinking was concerned with perception – not logic.

Logic will never change emotions and behaviour. Trying to persuade people logically to change emotions is useless in practice, and most people have experienced this. It is perceptions that control emotions and emotions control behaviour. Changes in perception will change emotions and therefore behaviour. If your perception changes, you have no choice: your emotions and behaviour change too.

THINKING SOFTWARE

Worldwide there are probably about 50,000 people writing software for computers. It is obvious that a computer cannot work without software. It is also obvious that new and more powerful software will allow the same computer to behave far more effectively.

How many people are writing software for the human brain?

The basic and traditional thinking software that we use was developed 2,400 years ago by the GG3. Who were the GG3? This was the Greek Gang of Three. They were Socrates, Plato and Aristotle.

Socrates was interested in asking questions (usually leading questions). He was also most interested in dialectic or argument.

Plato was interested in the ultimate 'truth' (he also considered democracy to be a silly system).

Aristotle created 'box logic'. Something was in this box or not and could never be half in and half out. Although he was married twice, he never asked either of his wives to open their mouths so he might count their teeth. He knew that men had more teeth in their mouths than women because with horses this was so. Creatures in the category of males (like horses) have more teeth than those in the category female – this was Aristotle-type logic.

The Renaissance and the Church

At the Renaissance, this wonderful Greek thinking spread across Europe. At that time schools, universities and thinking in general were in the hands of the Church.

The Church did not need creative thinking, or design thinking, or perceptual thinking, all of which I will discuss later. What the Church did need was argument, truth and logic with which to prove heretics wrong.

So argument, truth and logic became the core of our thinking in culture, in education and in the operations of society (such as law).

Creativity and inventiveness were left to individuals but never became part of education.

Argument, truth and logic proved so excellent in science and technology that we came to consider this thinking as perfect, complete and beyond any need for change.

Why have we not done more about software for human thinking?

Bookshops have a hard time deciding where to place my books. They get placed under Philosophy, Psychology, Business, Education and even Humour. There is no category for 'Thinking'.

There is no category called 'Thinking' in bookshops because we have always believed that thinking was well looked after by philosophy and psychology.

Imagine someone sitting at a table with a large sheet of white cardboard in front of him and a pair of scissors. With the scissors he cuts the cardboard into intricate shapes. Then he carefully puts all the pieces together again and smiles in triumph.

Philosophers do this. They describe the world in concepts, perceptions and values and then put these pieces together again.

Psychology arose from folk tales, myths, magic and astrology as a way of understanding people and predicting behaviour. But psychology understood that in order to become a real science there was a need for measurement. Measurement was the opposite of myth. So psychology became obsessed with measurement. Today, psychology is much concerned with putting people into boxes on the basis of some measurement.

Both philosophy and psychology are descriptive and analytical in nature. They are not operational. They do not provide practical tools for thinking.

So there should be a category called 'Thinking' because this is separate from philosophy, psychology and even mathematics.

I find it rather sad that when students who are interested in human thinking enter university, they choose to study philosophy. This is not about human thinking at all, and effectively sterilises their minds. I studied psychology at Oxford, but it was not an operational subject – it was just the history of psychology.

I am currently Da Vinci Professor of Thinking at the University of Advancing Technology in Arizona. I am also professor of thinking at four other universities. Very few universities have a Faculty of Thinking.

My interest in thinking has resulted in me designing practical operational tools and frameworks for thinking. These are now used by four-year-olds in school and by top executives at the world's largest corporations. Tools have to be simple, practical and effective. I am providing what philosophy and psychology have never provided. I am providing new software for human thinking.

The mechanism of mind

For the first time in human history we can base the design for human thinking on an understanding of how the human mind actually works.

I graduated as a medical doctor and worked in the field of medicine for 48 years. I was doing research in addition to clinical duties. I had teaching positions at the universities of Oxford, London, Cambridge and Harvard. I had also graduated separately in Psychology.

In medicine I was doing research into the interaction of various systems: respiratory, kidney, heart, glands, etc. If you can understand what is going on, you can design treatments.

I once had a patient with Idiopathic Postural Hypo-tension. This is a rare condition but, for those with it, these unfortunate people spent their whole lives lying flat in bed because, if they stood up, they fainted. Various approaches, including Air Force G-suits, had been tried without much success. I figured out that the arteriolar tone going to the kidneys was poor, so, when they lay down, the kidneys acted as if there was too much blood volume and got rid of the salt and water. So they never had enough blood – and collapsed.

The cure was very simple. No medication and no operations were needed. All that was required were two six-inch blocks of wood under the head of the bed – one on each side. The kidneys now acted as if there was *not enough blood* so they held on to the salt and water. The patients were now able to live a 100 per cent normal life.

If you understand the system you can design appro-priate action. That is what I did.

From my work in medicine I derived certain principles of 'self-organising systems'. I applied these principles to the neural network in the brain in order to understand how the mind worked.

In 1969 I wrote a book with the title *The Mechanism of Mind*. This book was read by the leading physicist in the world, Professor Murray Gell-Mann, who won his Nobel prize for discovering the quark. He also founded the Santa Fe Institute, which deals specifically with complex systems. He liked my book so much that he commissioned a team of computer experts to simulate what I had written in the book. They confirmed that the system I suggested for the brain behaved exactly as I had predicted. Two other computer teams, elsewhere in the world, have also confirmed this.

Professor Murray Gell-Mann has remained to this day a valued supporter of my ideas. It is interesting that when I am addressing groups of mathematicians or physicists, they fully understand and agree with what I am saying. They can understand the behaviour of self-organising systems like the human mind. All this is very far from the word games of traditional philosophy.

From this basis of understanding how the brain works I designed the formal and deliberate tools of Lateral Thinking. Later in this book I shall elaborate further on how the brain works.

I shall also show how the asymmetric patterning behaviour of the human brain gives rise to both creativity and humour.

For the first time in the history of the human race, we can relate ways of thinking, or software for the human brain, to how the information system of the brain actually works. This is very, very different from philosophers playing around with words and concepts but with no understanding of how the brain actually works. That is the difference.

WE HAVE SUCH EXCELLENT THINKING!

Is our thinking all bad? No! We have such excellent thinking, how can there be any suggestion that our thinking is inadequate?

Look at some successes:

- We can land men on the moon and watch them walk around in real time (Buzz Aldrin is actually a friend of mine).
- We can fly faster than the speed of sound (Concorde).
- We can pick up a mobile phone in Australia and get to talk to a particular person in the USA.
- We have computers, from the simplest to the most complex.
- We have devised the Internet, which connects up millions of people around the world.
- We have nuclear energy.
- Global television can send pictures and live stories around the world.
- We can transplant a human heart.
- In the past, pneumonia was often fatal. Today it is a minor ailment treated with a short course of antibiotics.
- Tuberculosis was a major cause of death less than a century ago. Today it has virtually been eliminated in developed countries.
- We can alter the very genes themselves of plants, animals and humans.
- We can clone animals (and soon people).
- We can store a huge amount of data on a tiny microchip.

These are but a small sample of our wonderful achievements. They are the results of excellent thinking.

Different

A scientist holds a piece of iron in his hands. The properties of iron are known, permanent, constant. He puts the iron together with something else and the result is technology.

You call someone an idiot. Immediately that person is offended, changes and is no longer the same person you called an idiot. In human affairs there are interactive loops. Things do not remain the same. Human affairs are unpredictable.

Then there is the huge importance of perception in human affairs. Perception is far more important than logic, but has been totally neglected.

So, unfortunately, our excellent thinking in scientific and technical matters does not carry over to other areas. But our pride in our thinking does carry over – with the unfortunate result of complacency.

Excellent – but not enough

We are very complacent and satisfied with the excellence of our thinking because we have produced great achievements in science, technology and engineering (space, mobile phones, medicines, etc.). Yet in other, more human, areas, we have made no progress at all. We still seek to solve conflicts with 'judgement' instead of designing the way forwards.

There is a chef who cooks an excellent omelette. It is the best omelette in the world. It cannot be faulted. The chef is no good at cooking anything else. Here we have excellence, but it is not enough.

The rear left wheel of a particular motor car is excellent. It cannot be faulted or attacked on any grounds. But that wheel by itself is not enough. If you believed that all you needed on a car was one wheel, there would be something wrong with your thinking – not with that rear left wheel. We also need the other wheels. The rear left wheel is excellent – but it is not enough.

An educated man speaks English flawlessly. But when he is in France, he finds that although his excellent English is still excellent, it is not enough.

I believe that our existing thinking methods are excellent when applied to certain areas, and inadequate (and even useless) in other areas.

If the English-speaking person in France speaks more loudly and more forcibly, this does not make him better understood. Insistence on traditional thinking does not make it more adequate.

If a diner wants something other than an omelette, the fact that the chef can create a perfect omelette is excellent but will not work for that diner.

These thinking methods are excellent, but not enough. I believe that our thinking culture, methods and habits are excellent. Like the rear left wheel they are excellent in themselves. But they are not enough. We need to supplement them with creative thinking, design thinking and perceptual thinking (among other things). Unfortunately, our existing traditional thinking habits insist that you must attack something and show it to be bad before you can suggest a change. It is much more difficult to acknowledge that something is excellent and then to ask for change because although it is excellent, it is not enough.

MY THINKING

Throughout this book I shall use the term 'my thinking' to refer to any of the thinking methods and software that I have designed. This is simpler than spelling out in each case the particular method that is in use. To use just the word 'thinking' would be misleading, because it might be understood as referring to traditional thinking, critical thinking, and so on. The term 'my thinking' refers directly to the new thinking methods I have designed.

Many readers will know of my work in lateral thinking and may assume that all references are to this method. This is not the case. There are several other methods. There is the exploratory method of the Six Hats and parallel thinking (instead of argument). There is the perceptual thinking of the CoRT (Cognitive Research Trust) method designed for schools (some of the basic tools of which are designed in more detail later in Chapter 10). There are also programmes for simplicity and value scanning. All these methods and more come under the term 'my thinking'.

There are times when my thinking is totally different from, and even contrary to, traditional logic (for example, with provocation). In general, however, I have no quarrel with traditional thinking. I merely think it is incomplete and inadequate in some areas. I would like to see my methods used to supplement traditional thinking – not to replace it.

How new thinking has worked

Over the last 40 years I have worked in 73 countries. These have been mainly seminars and lectures with some conferences and meetings.

I have taught thinking to four-year-olds and 90-year-olds (Roosevelt University has a special programme for seniors). I have taught thinking to top business executives and illiterate miners. I have taught thinking to Down's Syndrome youngsters and to Nobel Laureates. I once lectured to 8,000 Mormons in Salt Lake City. In Christchurch, New Zealand, I lectured for 90 minutes to 7,400 children (aged six to 12) who had been brought together by mayoress Vicki Buck.

Over the years I have been invited to talk to a large number of business corporations including BA, BAA, Bank of America, Barclays, BP, Citicorp, Ericsson, Exxon, Ford, GM, IBM, Kuwait Oil, Microsoft, Motorola, Nokia, Philips, Shell, UBS and many others. I have also been invited to talk to government departments, cabinet offices, and so on.

In my experience, even the most rigid and authoritarian regimes welcome new thinking. I have given seminars in China many times and they are currently trying out my work in schools. Elsewhere in the world, the programme is widely used: in Australia, New Zealand, Singapore, Malaysia, India (increasingly) and Canada. There is patchy use as well in the UK, USA, Ireland, Italy and Malta.

Below are some small examples of where my thinking (new thinking) has made a difference. These examples do not prove anything – they merely provide a perspective.

- In the old days of the Soviet Union, I was on a visit to Moscow to lecture at various departments of the Academy of Sciences. I was also invited to a meeting of the Foreign Affairs committee of the Politburo. The chairman of the meeting had in front of him my book on conflict resolution, *Conflicts*. There were notes in the margin and underlinings. He saw me looking at the book and said, 'This is not Gorbachev's copy – he has his own.' I was later told by a senior politician from Kazakhstan that, in those days of perestroika, my books were top reading in the Kremlin.

- John Buchanan, the former coach of the Australian national cricket team, came to see me to ask me to train his team in thinking. I gave them a short seminar.

In their next encounter with the English team, they not only won easily, they inflicted the biggest defeat in the history of Test cricket. I had a note from John Buchanan acknowledging my contribution.

- One of my trainers, Caroline Ferguson, was working with a steel company in South Africa. One afternoon she set up some workshops to generate new ideas. Using just one of the tools of lateral thinking (random input), they generated 21,000 ideas in a single afternoon. It took them nine months just to sort through the ideas.

- The Hungerford Guidance Centre in London works with youngsters who are deemed to be too violent to be taught in ordinary schools: they have stabbed a teacher, for example, or set a school on fire. More than 20 years ago, the principal, David Lane, started teaching my ways of thinking to these violent youngsters. He has now done a 20-year follow-up and has shown that the actual rate of criminal conviction for those taught thinking is less than one-tenth of that for those not taught thinking. This statistic is a fact.

- A school in Argentina teaches my thinking very thoroughly. In the national examinations, they did so much better than all the other schools that they were investigated for cheating!

- As a student, Ashok Chouhan was travelling from India to Europe. He had three dollars in his pocket. His plane was diverted to Paris. He had some time at the airport and went into the bookshop. He bought a copy of my first book (in English). At an evening lecture I was giving in Delhi, he told me he kept this book in his briefcase for 30 years. Today he has $3 billion in his pocket; he founded Amity University in India; and he was, at one time, the largest investor in East Germany. He believes that 80 per cent of his success was triggered by that book.

- I was once giving a seminar in Barcelona. After the seminar a man from the island of Tenerife came up to me. He told me that when he was younger he had not been any good at school subjects. Then he read one of my books – I do not know which one. Today he owns seven companies in Holland and Spain.

- The Olympic Games in Montreal in 1976 lost a great deal of money (perhaps $1 billion). After Montreal, no city in the world wanted to host the games. Eventually, Moscow agreed to host the games in 1980. After Moscow, again no city wanted the games. Finally Los Angeles agreed to host the games. Instead of a loss, they made a profit of $250 million. As a result of this, today every city wants the games and competes to get them (there have even been allegations of bribery where cities are desperate). When Peter Ueberroth, the organiser of the LA games, was interviewed in the *Washington Post*, he attributed his success to his ability to generate new ideas through the use of my lateral thinking and he gave examples. I wrote and asked him where he had learned this. He reminded me that he had been my host in 1975 at a 90-minute lecture I had given to the YPO (Young Presidents Organisation) in Boca Raton, Florida. From that 90 minutes he had remembered enough to use the processes effectively nine years later.

• I was on the Innovations Council of the State of Victoria in Australia. After a meeting of the council, Professor Doherty came up to me to tell me how he had read my first book. This had changed his thinking and, as a result, he won the Nobel Prize.

• The Atkey organisation is an independent organisation that, for several years, has been introducing my work into schools in the United Kingdom and doing research. They have shown that teaching my thinking as a separate subject increases performance in every other subject by between 30 and 100 per cent.

• A town council that had been taught my methods by Vicki Cavins reported that in the first year they had saved $84 million on a single project.

- Unemployed youngsters on the New Deal scheme in the United Kingdom were taught my thinking for just five hours by the Holst Group. The employment rate among those taught increased 500 per cent. A year later, 96 per cent of those were still in employment. This was more successful than anything that had been done before.

- In Australia, Jennifer O'Sullivan was in charge of two job clubs, which were made up of groups of unemployed youngsters. The normal rate of employment out of such clubs was 40 per cent. She taught them my thinking and she got 70 per cent employment out of one club and 100 per cent out of the other. And every one of her youngsters was completely deaf.

- I have been told that Siemens (the largest corporation in Europe) has reduced product development time by 50 per cent by using my thinking.

There are many such examples. I have written these things to show that there has been a lot of experience with these methods. They are easy to teach, easy to use and very practical. If nothing else, the books I have written reassure people that their unusual thinking is perfectly valid.

Boasting

William James is my favourite philosopher, because he was concerned with pragmatism. To paraphrase one of his sayings: 'You can describe something this way or that. In the end, what matters is the cash value.' He did not mean actual money, but practical value. What this means is that there can be many complex descriptions and theories. But in the end, what practical difference do they make?

So the practical examples of the use of my thinking scattered throughout the book are essential, even if they do seem like boasting. They show that these things work in real life: in business, in education, and so on.

I was once interviewed by a journalist who said that she did not want to hear about these practical effects of my work. You can imagine how useless the published interview must have seemed.

A Canadian educator once declared that my CoRT programme was so simple it could not possibly work. I told him that this was like saying that cheese did not exist – because the method does work, with strong results.

1 Creativity

We need to look closely at the ways in which our thinking doesn't work. I will be covering a different area of our thinking in each of Chapters 1 to 14. I am going to start with creativity because creativity is a huge deficiency in our thinking habits. We know very well that progress is due to creativity: to looking at things in a different way; to doing things differently; to putting things together to deliver new values.

We rely on creativity. We depend on creativity. Yet all we have been able to do is to hope that certain creative individuals will supply us with new ideas and new possibilities.

WHY WE NEED CREATIVITY

The human brain is not designed to be creative. It is designed to set up routine patterns and to use and follow these patterns. That is why life is practical and possible.

We may need to use routine patterns 98 per cent of the time and only to be creative 2 per cent of the time.

To show this, there is a game where you start with a letter and then add another letter. At each point, as you add another letter, a whole word has to be formed.

Start with 'a'.

Add 't'. The new word is 'at'.

Add 'c'. The new word is 'cat'.

Add 'o'. The new word is 'coat'.

Add 'r'. The new word is 'actor'.

Until the addition of the 'r' it was quite simple to add the new letter to the existing ones to form a new word. With the 'r' it was necessary to go back and completely restructure the use of the previous words.

We live over time. New information comes in over time. We add this new information to what we already have. There may come a point where we have to go back and restructure what we had before. This is creativity. More often we are not forced to go back. We stick to what we have. If, however, we choose to go back and restructure then we get a much better arrangement. This is creativity we choose to use.

COMMODITIES AND VALUES

Technology is becoming a commodity. Everyone can have access to it. Manufacturing processes and efficiencies are also becoming a commodity available to everyone.

China and India are rapidly developing as manu-facturing countries – and at a much lower cost.

In a free-trade world the only differentiator is going to be creativity. With creativity you use the commodities to deliver new products, new services and new values.

Creativity is needed to offer new values through new products and new services. Creativity can also design new and better ways of delivering old and established values. Creativity can also design new values directly – and then find ways of delivering these new values.

LANGUAGE PROBLEM

There is a language problem with our understanding of the word 'creativity'. As we understand it, if you create something that was not there before, then you are creative. But this may not necessarily be a good thing. You may have just created a mess.

This leads to the notion that creativity is just being different for the sake of being different – which is what far too many creative people believe.

If doors are normally rectangular and you suggest a triangular door, that is not creative unless you can show value for the new shape.

The problem then is that the word 'creative' does not distinguish between artistic creativity – as we understand it – and idea creativity, which helps with our thinking. That the result is something new is enough for us to term it 'creativity'. That is why it was necessary to invent the term 'lateral thinking' to refer specifically to idea creativity.

Although my thinking is quite widely used in the artistic world (especially in music), I am writing here about *idea creativity*.

Idea creativity

Because there is no specific word in the English language for 'idea creativity' there is the possibility of dangerous confusion. Schools claim that they are indeed teaching 'creativity' when they are teaching some music, dancing and finger painting.

Many people believe that, if you create a mess, then you have created something new and, theoretically, you are therefore 'creative'. The production of something that was not there before implies creation without any regard to the value of that creation. Indeed, many people have come to believe that being different for the sake of being different is the essence of creativity.

There is a need in our language for a word that emphasises idea creativity, and that also indicates change, newness and value.

REASONS

There are a number of reasons why we have done nothing culturally, academically, etc., about creativity.

There is the language problem mentioned above. This leads to problems with understanding. If you claim to be able to teach people creativity, you are asked if you could ever teach someone to be a Leonardo da Vinci or a Ludwig van Beethoven, a Claude Monet or a Frédéric Chopin. Since this is unlikely, the conclusion is that creativity cannot be taught.

Since creativity cannot be explained or achieved logically, it must be some mysterious talent that only some people have and others can only envy.

All creative ideas will be logical in hindsight – that is, after you have come up with the idea, if the idea is indeed logical in hindsight, then it will be claimed that logic should have reached the idea in the first place. So creativity is unnecessary because logic is enough. The complete nonsense of this attitude in an asymmetric system will be explained later.

Intelligence is not enough for creativity. So intelligent people defend the position given them by their intelligence by claiming that creativity is not a learnable skill but an inborn talent – which they cannot be expected to acquire.

These are some of the traditional reasons why we have paid very little attention to creativity.

BRAINSTORMING FOR CREATIVITY

This method originated in the advertising industry as a formal approach to creativity. It has some value, but overall it is very weak.

Imagine a person walking down the road. This is an ordinary person – not a musician. This person is then tied up with a rope. Someone now produces a violin. Obviously the person tied up with the rope cannot play the violin. It is then suggested that if the rope is cut, the person will be able to play the violin; to become a violinist. This is obviously nonsense, but it is similar to what happens in brainstorming – simply removing inhibitions (as in cutting the rope) is not enough.

If you are inhibited and if people attack every one of your ideas, then creativity is indeed difficult. So if we remove the inhibition and we remove the attacks, surely everyone will be creative. This has a little bit more logic than cutting the rope in the above example because it assumes that everyone has some creative talent.

Brainstorming does have a value, but it is a very weak process compared with some of the formal tools of lateral thinking. Just removing inhibitions and suspending judgement is not enough. The traditional process of brainstorming sometimes gives the impression of shooting out a stream of (often crazy) ideas in the hope that one of them might hit a useful target.

There is a need for more deliberate processes to encourage and enhance creativity actively.

CREATIVITY: TALENT OR SKILL?

This is a very fundamental question. If creativity is an inborn talent then we can search for that talent, nurture it, develop it and encourage it. But there is nothing we can do for those who do not have this inborn talent.

I remind you that I am writing about idea creativity and lateral thinking rather than artistic talent.

If idea creativity is a skill then everyone can learn this skill, practise it and apply it. As with any skill, such as tennis, skiing and cooking, some people will be better at the skill than others. Everyone, however, can acquire a usable level of the skill. Idea creativity can be taught and used as formally as mathematics.

BEHAVIOUR

There are some people who do seem to be more creative than others. This is because they enjoy and value creativity. As a result they spend more time trying to be creative. They build up confidence in their creative abilities. All this does is make them more creative. It is a positive feedback system.

Some people seem more curious than others. Some people seem to enjoy creativity and new ideas more than others.

This does not mean that those who do not have this temperament cannot be creative. They can learn the deliberate skills of lateral thinking just as they might learn the basic skills of mathematics. Everyone can learn to add up numbers and multiply them.

The argument that creativity cannot be taught is usually based on pointing to extreme cases of creativity and talent, such as Einstein, Michelangelo, Bjorn Borg. But imagine a row of people lined up to run a race. The starting signal is given and the race is run. Someone comes first and someone comes last. Their performance depended on their natural running ability.

Now if all the runners have some training on roller skates, they all finish the race much faster than before. However, someone still comes first and someone still comes last.

So if we do nothing about creativity then obviously creative ability depends only on 'natural' talent. But if we provide training, structures and systematic techniques, then we raise the general level of creative ability. Some people will be much better than others but everyone will acquire some creative skill.

Then how is this skill to be acquired? Exhortation and example do have some effect, but only a weak one. There is a need for specific mental tools, operations and habits, which lead to creative new ideas. These tools and techniques can be learned, practised and used in a deliberate manner.

It is no longer a matter of sitting by a stream and listening to Baroque music and hoping for the inspiration of a new idea. You can try that, by all means, but it is far less effective than the deliberate use of a lateral thinking technique.

As you acquire skill in the techniques, you develop more confidence and the result is that you get better and better ideas.

All the lateral thinking tools are designed on the basis of understanding the brain as a self-organising information system that forms asymmetric patterns. Over 40 years of use, the tools have been shown to be effective across a wide range of ages, abilities, backgrounds and cultures. This is because the tools are so fundamental. This is because the tools affect behaviour.

THE LOGIC OF CREATIVITY

It may surprise many people to learn that idea creativity is a logical process, because they believe that logic can never achieve creativity. Creativity is indeed logical, but it is a very different sort of logic.

Logic defines the rules of behaviour within a certain universe. With our normal logic, the universe is one of language or discrete elements: language refers to separate things like box, cloud, smile, etc. These are discrete or separated elements. With creativity, the universe is that of a self-organising patterning system that makes asymmetric patterns. Logic defines the rules of behaviour within this rather special universe.

Patterns

One morning a fellow gets up and realises he has 11 items of clothing to put on. In how many ways can he get dressed?

He sets his computer to work through all the ways of getting dressed. The computer takes 40 hours to go through all the ways (this was tested some years ago; today's computers will be faster but the concept is the same). With 11 items of clothing, there are 39,916,800 ways of getting dressed.

There are 11 choices for the first item, 10 choices for the next, and so on.

If you were to spend just one minute concentrating on each way of getting dressed, you would need to live to the age of 76 years old – using every minute of your waking life trying ways of getting dressed.

Life would be impractical and rather difficult if the brain worked that way. You would take forever to get up in the morning, cross the road, get to work, read and write.

But the brain does not work that way. We exist because the brain is a self-organising information system that allows patterns to form from incoming information. That is its excellence. All we then need to do is to recognise the routine 'getting dressed' pattern, switch into it and go through that normal routine. That is why you can drive to work in the morning, read, write, and all the other things you do in your day-to-day life.

Imagine you have a piece of paper and you make marks with a pen on that surface. The surface records the marks accurately. Previous marks do not affect the way a new mark is received.

Change the surface to a shallow dish of gelatin. You now put spoonfuls of hot water on to the gelatin. The hot water dissolves the gelatin. In time, channels are formed in the surface. In this case previous information strongly affects the way new information is received. The process is no different from rain falling on a landscape. Streams are formed and then rivers. New rain is channelled along the tracks formed by preceding rain. The gelatin and landscape have allowed the hot water and rain to organise themselves into channels or sequences.

In my 1969 book *The Mechanism of Mind* I showed how the brain, unlike computers, is this second type of information-receiving surface. I showed how neural networks act like the gelatin or the landscape.

What is a pattern?
There is a pattern whenever the change from one state to the next one has a higher chance of happening in one direction than in any other. If you are standing on a path

in a garden, the chances of you proceeding another step down the path are much more likely than of you wandering off the path.

How the brain forms patterns is described in my book *The Mechanism of Mind*.

We can even represent a pattern by that path. At each moment we are more likely to take the next step in one direction than move down the path in any other direction. Under given circumstances a certain 'state' in the brain is more likely to be followed by one particular other state than by any other.

Asymmetry

Patterning systems tend to be asymmetric, though.

As above, we can represent a pattern by a path, since at every next step the highest probability is to move along the path rather than stop and consider every side track. Point A is at the beginning of the path towards point B; point C is at the end of a side track. All this means is that the route from A to C is not the same as the route from C to A. You can go from A to C (you follow the usual routine or path towards B and in a roundabout way you come round to the other end of the side track, i.e. C) whereas, if you were to enter the side track from another point at point C, route C to A is very straightforward (you go straight down the side track to the main path or route).

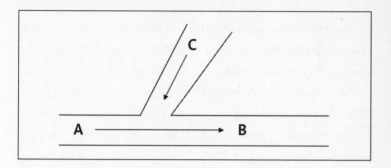

Consider instead that the main path from point A then narrowed to a point D. The narrowing of the track means that, while going from A to D is difficult, the reverse is not so difficult. Then the path from A to B is wide open in comparison so the possibility of taking the track to D is remote.

This asymmetry is the logical basis for both humour and creativity.

HUMOUR AND CREATIVITY

Humour is by far the most significant behaviour of the human brain, far more significant than reason. Humour tells us more about the underlying system. Humour tells us that the brain makes asymmetric patterns.

In humour, we are led along the main path from A and then suddenly we are shifted to the end of the side path (B) and immediately we see the track we might have taken (from B to A). Once there, we can see that it actually makes sense and is perfectly logical.

For example, an old man of 90 goes down to hell. Wandering around, he sees a friend of his of a similar age. Sitting on the knee of this friend is a beautiful young blonde.

He says to his friend: 'Are you sure this is hell? You seem to be having rather a good time!'

The friend replies: 'It is hell all right. I am the punishment for her.'

The explanation is perfectly logical but reverses the situation completely. That is the surprise of humour.

An Englishman on a railway station in Ireland storms into the stationmaster's office to complain that on the platform there are two clocks each showing a different time.

The stationmaster looks at him and says: 'To be sure, and what would be the use of having two clocks if they showed the same time?' There is an unexpected logic in the reply. It is the surprise element of suddenly switching perceptions that makes us laugh.

Two blondes are walking along a canal, one on each side of the canal. One blonde calls out to the other, 'How do I get to the other side?' The other blonde replies, 'But you are already on the other side.'

Humour derives part of its effect by bringing in various prejudices and preconceptions.

Returning to my seat on an aeroplane I hit my head on the overhead luggage locker. The person next to me said, 'I also hit my head on that locker. It must be too low.'

'On the contrary,' I said, 'the trouble is that the locker is placed too high, not too low.'

There is nothing humorous about this exchange but there is the same sudden switch in perception, which eventually makes sense. If the luggage locker were placed really low, you would realise you must duck your head. If the locker were placed really high, it would not matter whether you ducked or not. If the locker is placed at a level that suggests you do not need to duck, you do not duck and you hit your head.

The humour model of the asymmetric pattern is also the model for creativity. You suddenly see something differently and it makes sense in hindsight.

All valuable creative ideas will be logical in hindsight. In a sense, the definition of 'valuable' means logical in hindsight.

For the first time in human history we have a logical basis for creativity. Creativity is no longer a mysterious gift or special talent. We can now see creativity as the behaviour of a self-organising information system that makes asymmetric patterns (the brain).

Once we can understand the underlying system, then we can design tools for the deliberate use of creativity. These tools can be very powerful. It need no longer be a matter of sitting and waiting for ideas and inspiration. We can do certain things that will result in the brain having new ideas. This is a big step forwards in the history of mankind.

Being without this for 2,400 years has caused immense problems and explains why we have done nothing about creativity.

If an idea is 'logical' in hindsight, then we claim that it could have been obtained by 'logic' in the first place. So we do not need creativity because all such ideas should have been reached by logic.

This is complete and perfect nonsense. In an asymmetric system what is obvious and logical in hindsight may be inaccessible in foresight.

Because philosophers have been playing with words and not considered self-organising pattern-making systems they have not been able to see that obvious in hindsight is not at all obvious in foresight. That is why we have done nothing about creativity.

THE RANDOM WORD TOOL FOR CREATIVITY

This was the tool that generated over 20,000 new ideas for a steel company in a single afternoon from a workshop. I have chosen this lateral thinking tool first for a number of reasons.

1. It seems totally illogical and unlikely to work.
2. It may be the easiest of the tools to use.
3. It is very powerful.
4. It is actually totally logical.

Process

You have your focus. You know where you want to generate new ideas.

You then obtain a 'random word'. Nouns are easiest to use, so use a noun. You can obtain your random word in several ways.

You may keep a list of 60 words on a card in your pocket. You then glance at your watch. If the second hand shows 27 seconds, you select word number 27 from your list.

You could also choose a page number in a dictionary and then specify the tenth (or other) word down on that page. You continue downwards until you come to a noun. You could do this with any book with a page and line number.

You could put words written on slips of paper into a bag and then pick one out.

You could close your eyes and stab your finger at a page of a newspaper or book. You take the word nearest to your finger.

All of these are practical ways of obtaining a random word. Once you have your random word, you then use this random word to generate ideas about the subject. This is a mental operation called 'movement' and quite different from 'judgement', which I describe elsewhere. The task is to use the random word to open up new lines of thinking. It is not a matter of finding a connection between the random word and the subject.

Logic

At first sight the process seems totally illogical. The essence of logic is that what comes next is relevant and related to what is being considered. With the random word technique, what comes next is completely irrelevant and unrelated.

If a random word is truly random then it will be equally related to any possible focus. Indeed, any random word will be related to any focus. Logicians would point out that this is complete nonsense. Yet it is totally logical – in the universe of asymmetric patterning systems. I shall explain the logic in more detail elsewhere, but here is a simple explanation.

You live in a small town and when you leave home you always take the main road, which satisfies your travel needs. There are many side roads that you ignore. One day your car breaks down on the outskirts of the town and you have to walk home. You ask around for instructions. You find yourself arriving home by a route you have never taken before. You note that this is a much better way of getting to your favourite restaurant. The logic is simple. If you start from the centre, your path is determined by the pattern probabilities at that point – so you take the familiar route. If you have a different starting point at the periphery and make your way to the centre you open up a new route.

Shaping

Shaping is a broad term, which covers influencing, changing, concept transfer, effect, etc.

You are trying to get some new ideas for a restaurant. You use the random-word technique. The word is 'cinema'.

The shaping could be very direct. Diners could order a DVD player and earphones and watch a movie as they ate. Some couples have more need to eat than to talk.

The shaping could be more indirect. Cinemas are usually in darkness. So a rather dark restaurant where you might appreciate more the taste of the food. And it would not matter who you were with as no one could see. From that we could move on to a very discreet restaurant where each couple had its own private cubicle.

Cinemas have set times to show a movie. Maybe a restaurant could have different menus at different times so you chose your time according to the menu you preferred.

How might the word 'bible' shape 'exams'?

The bible is unchanging so perhaps the questions in an exam would always be the same. Each question, however, would be designed to test the candidates' knowledge of the subject.

The bible is about 'truth'. So perhaps exams would allow candidates to reply in two distinct ways. There would be the 'truth reply' and then there would be the 'speculative reply' signalled as such.

THE RANDOM WORD EFFECT

Considering asymmetry it is easy to see why the lateral thinking 'random word' tool works.

The random word comes in from direction C. This has two effects. The first is that the dominance of the A to B path is avoided. The second is that the new direction of C is opened up.

The random word is not the idea itself. The random word is not itself 'C'. The random word opens up the path, which can lead to the idea at C.

So the random word is a perfectly logical procedure in the universe of asymmetric patterns.

Lateral thinking implies moving sideways and changing perceptions, concepts, starting points, etc., instead of just working harder with the existing ones. In the tennis example in Chapter 4, you shift attention from the winner to the losers to get out of the usual line of thought.

In another example, Granny is sitting knitting. Susan, who is three years old, is upsetting Granny by playing with her ball of wool. One parent suggests that Susan should be put in the playpen to prevent her from annoying Granny. The other parent suggests that Granny should be put in the playpen to protect her from Susan.

On a more technical level, the asymmetry example shows that lateral thinking implies moving across patterns instead of just along them. So we move laterally from the main path to the end of the side track. Once found, it will be logical in hindsight.

Exercise

Four focus subjects are given below, along with a list of 60 random words. Obtain a random word for each. Tackle the different subjects on different occasions – not all at once.

Focus:

A new television show

A new type of sport

A new idea for a motor car

A new idea for an Internet business

Random words

Look at the second hand of your watch to determine which numbered random word to use.

Letter	Barrier	Ear
Tooth	Bomb	Soap
Parachute	Fireworks	Spectacles
Nail	Wheel	Key
Cup	Police	Bible
Wallet	Scream	Paint
Cabbage	Cloud	Swim
Worm	Radio	Wine
Traffic	Beach	Pension
Ticket	Flowers	Circus
Balloon	Code	Rubber
Desk	Licence	School

Tower	Pill	Axe
Office	Soup	Ring
Tennis	Bed	Shop
Race	Flea	Eye
Moon	Net	Law
Gate	Chain	Exam
Chair	Bus	Bread
Beer	Boat	Club

SUMMARY: CREATIVITY

In creativity, the process is the same as with humour. We suddenly see something differently, move laterally to the side track and find that in hindsight it makes complete sense. But how do we get to the 'idea point' on the side track? That is precisely where the techniques of provocation come in. They are methods of helping us to escape from the main track in order to increase our chances of getting to the side track – the 'lateral' of lateral thinking refers to moving sideways across the patterns instead of moving along them as in normal thinking.

Using lateral thinking, I put forward a provocation. I invented the word 'po' to signal that what followed was intended as a provocation. 'Po' could mean (P)rovocative (O)peration. What followed was to be used for its 'movement' value, not for its 'judgement' value. The provocations may be totally unreasonable. With provocation, we can be temporarily 'mad' for just 30 seconds at a time in a controllable fashion. Judgement would have to reject such ideas as nonsense. Movement can move on from such ideas to useful new ideas, which is why provocation is such a fundamental aspect of lateral thinking and creativity in general.

I was giving a seminar to an environmental group in California. Someone mentioned the problem of a factory on a river putting out pollution so that people downstream suffered from this pollution. So I suggested the provocation: 'Po the factory is downstream of itself.'

The provocation sounds totally impossible – it is what is called a 'wishful-thinking' provocation. The idea is totally ridiculous because the factory cannot be in two places at once. But, using 'movement', we extract the concept that 'the factory should suffer from its own pollution'. From that comes a very simple idea: we legislate that, when you build a factory on a river, your water input must always be downstream of your own polluted output. So you would be the first to suffer from your pollution. I have been told that this has now become legislation in some countries.

The idea is totally logical in hindsight, as are most creative ideas.

But the idea cannot be reached by logic, because of the asymmetric nature of patterns. Those who claim that if an idea is logical in hindsight then it must be attainable by logic in the first place simply do not understand asymmetric patterns.

A tree trunk splits into two. Then each trunk splits again into branches, which in turn split again. What are the chances of an ant on the trunk of the tree reaching a specified leaf? At each branch point the chances diminish by one over the number of branches; in an average tree, the chances would be about 1:8,000.

Now imagine the ant on a particular leaf. What are the chances of that ant reaching the trunk of the tree? The chances are 1:1, or 100 per cent. There are no forward branches in that direction. That is asymmetry.

In the same way, the chances of reaching a creative idea through logic may be very slight. But once the idea has been reached, it is obvious and logical in hindsight. That is the nature of asymmetric patterning systems – but no amount of word play will ever make us understand this point.

Creativity is important and becoming ever more important.

Exhortation has some value but not much. Just telling people to be creative is not enough.

Creativity is usable as a deliberate skill – it is no longer just waiting for ideas to happen.

2 The Formal Tools of Lateral Thinking

The word 'lateral' in relation to thinking means moving across patterns instead of moving along them – that is the nature and the logic of creativity.

There are formal tools that help us to move laterally, which can be learned and used deliberately just as we might learn and use mathematics. Some people will be more skilled in the use of these tools and will generate more ideas – but anyone can learn and use the tools. The tools greatly increase the chance of having new ideas – like the 21,000 new ideas generated in one afternoon in the steel mill through the use of just one of these tools.

Some people object that being creative means being free, and therefore any structure impedes creativity. That is incorrect. If you are in a locked room, you need a formal key to get out of the room. This key does not determine where you go once you are outside. Structure is your key.

Full understanding of these tools can be obtained by reading other books of mine, or through formal training. There are also about 1,200 certified lateral thinking trainers around the world, and many corporations now have internal trainers.

CHALLENGE

If there is an obvious and attractive route in one direction, we are blocked from taking other, unknown routes. The path leads us that way and we don't explore the edges or beyond. As discussed in Chapter 1, in the same way, the dominant pattern set-up in the mind takes us quickly in that direction.

The first of the lateral thinking tools requires that we block this obvious path (from A to B). It is very important to note that this block is never a criticism. The block acknowledges: 'This may be the best way – it may even be the only possible way. But for the moment we are going to block it and seek alternatives.'

It is very important that 'challenge' is never used as an attack. This is because we must be able to challenge even the best and most successful ideas. Otherwise we would be limited to dealing with imperfect ideas.

Oil wells were normally drilled vertically. This had been the method for over 80 years, and it worked very well. There was no problem with it. At a seminar for Shell Oil in London in 1970, I suggested, as the result of a challenge, that at a certain depth the drilling might proceed horizontally. Today this is standard procedure, and such wells produce between three and six times as much oil as the vertical wells. I am not claiming that this change was the result of my suggestion, but the idea turned out to work very well.

Why had it taken so long to develop this idea? While the original idea worked, there was no impetus to look for an alternative.

FOCUS

'We are all very creative. Now, what shall we be creative about?'

Focus is a very important part of applied creativity. Where do we want new ideas? If you cannot define your focus, you cannot generate ideas deliberately. You would just have to wait for ideas to arise by chance.

There are two broad types of focus.

Purpose focus

This is the type of focus with which we are most familiar. There is a problem that has to be solved. There is a process to be simplified. There is a task to be achieved. There is a conflict to be resolved. There is an improvement to be made, etc.

We know the clear purpose of our thinking. We know why we are thinking and what we hope to achieve. With purpose focus it is always possible to state the purpose very clearly. It is like travelling towards a destination. You know where you want to get to.

Area focus

This is very different from purpose focus. We simply define the 'area' where we want the new ideas, not the purpose for the ideas.

'We want some new ideas regarding the first steps someone takes when entering a bank.'
'We want some new ideas about car parks.'
'We want some new ideas about wine glasses.'
'We want some new ideas in the area of school lessons.'
'We want some new ideas about pencils.'

The new ideas about pencils may make pencils cheaper. A new idea may make pencils easier to sharpen. A new idea may add another function to pencils. A new idea may make pencils more attractive. A new idea may simplify the manufacture of pencils, etc.

For this focus the random word tool is particularly useful because it works even when there is no defined starting point.

The area defined as the focus may be broad or very narrow. You might say:

'I want new ideas about public transport.'

'I want new ideas about buses.'

'I want new ideas about bus routes.'

'I want new ideas about the seats in buses.'

'I want new ideas about the first seat in buses.'

All these focuses are usable.

What they need is the willingness of a person or people to pause and to focus on a point and then set out to do some lateral thinking. At this moment no specific techniques might be involved. What is needed is the investment of time, effort and focus – the will to find a new idea.

Once at a reception in Melbourne in Australia I met a young man, John Bertrand. Bertrand had been the skipper of the 1983 Australian challenge for the America's Cup yacht race. The Cup had only ever been won by America for 130 years, so John Bertrand told me how he and his crew had focused on point after point on their boat and set out to find new ideas of how to do it. By investing this time, effort and focus, the most obvious change they made was the design of the (now famous) winged keel. For the first time in history, the America's Cup was taken away from the United States. This is a classic example of the will to find new ideas, the will to use lateral thinking.

The creative hit list

This is a formal target list of focuses that need creative thinking. The list would be available on bulletin boards.

The list could be available on a website. The list could be printed on cards put on every desk or in every workplace.

Many creative people sit around waiting for ideas. The Creative Hit List provides a target and a demand. You are expected to have ideas about the items on the list. You may even be specifically asked to have an idea on a particular item by a particular date. A team may be assigned a task from the list and asked to report back on a given date.

The list may be changed but some items may be more permanent. There should be about 10 items on the list.

The items on the list would be a mixture of purpose focuses and also area focuses. People can also make suggestions as to new focuses that might be added to the list. The list provides a permanent 'demand' for creative effort.

An executive may attend a conference or read an article and realise that something he comes across is very relevant to an item on the Creative Hit List.

The Creative Hit List does not exclude specific creative tasks that might be assigned to individuals or a team. The List provides a permanent background demand that emphasises that creativity is always needed.

CONCEPTS

Concepts are a very important part of thinking in general and an even more important part of creative thinking.

It is interesting that the North American culture is not very keen on concepts. They are seen as academic abstractions contrasted with the 'hands-on action' that is needed. Yet concepts are essential for creativity.

You can identify the concept that seems to be in use and then seek to find other ways of delivering the same concept. If you understand the concept of car insurance, how else could you deliver that value? Perhaps with an insurance tax on petrol sales.

There can be operational or functional concepts. These describe the way something is done.

There can be value concepts. Why this is of value.

There can be purpose concepts. Why we are doing this.

There can be descriptive concepts covering a whole range of things that seem to have something in common.

There are usually several levels of concept ranging from the very broad to a concept that is so detailed it is almost an idea. An idea is a practical way of putting a concept into action.

On a very broad level, a bicycle is a means of transport. On the next level, a bicycle is a personal means of transport. On the next level, a bicycle is a human-powered (non-polluting) means of transport. On a more detailed level, a bicycle is a two-wheeled mechanism in which a pedal crank powers one of the wheels. After that comes the specific design of a bicycle.

Concepts breed ideas. From the concept of a personal, people-powered form of transport we can move on to alternatives, such as roller blades, skateboards or even completely new ideas like having the person inside a big wheel. Ways of attaching people to moving cars might also qualify. There might even be the idea of an electric motorcycle where you yourself charged up the battery at home using a treadmill generator.

Concept extraction

This lateral thinking technique should be easier to use than the others because it seems more 'reasonable'. In practice, it is rather hard to use because it does not have the direct provocative effect of the other techniques.

The importance of concepts has been discussed above. We seek to develop alternatives and new ideas by 'extracting the concept' and then looking around for other ways to deliver this concept by means of a specific idea.

Suppose we extracted from restaurants the concept of 'eating what you could purchase'. From this, might come the idea of phoning a number and ordering a cook, who would come, with food, and cook for you. Home delivery of food is another idea that is already in use. There might even be a system of meal invitations where an ordinary household invited a stranger to dinner at an established price.

In Australia, the mayor of a small town came to see me and told me that they had a problem with commuters who drove into the town and left their cars in the street all day. This made it impossible for people to find places to park if they wanted to go shopping. The normal solution was to put in parking meters in order to limit parking. Should he do this? It would be expensive to set up and to run.

What was the concept here? There was a need to find a way to limit the time people could leave their cars parked in the street. Another way would be to legislate that if you parked your car in certain designated areas, you had to leave your headlights full on. You could not leave your car there for very long because you would be running your battery down. There was no way you could leave your car there all day. You could only park, rush into a shop, then rush out and drive off. There was a self-imposed limit.

The concept fan

Within the concept, there is also 'the concept fan'.

You want to attach something to the ceiling in a room of normal height. The solution is simple. You look for a ladder. But you cannot find a ladder. Do you give up and decide that the task cannot be done?

A ladder is only one way of 'raising me off the ground'. 'Raising me off the ground' is the concept, the fixed point. There are alternative ways of satisfying this fixed point – standing on a table, or having people lift me up.

But 'raising me off the ground' is only one way of 'reducing the distance between the object and the ceiling'. This becomes the new fixed point and we look for alternatives for this.

These alternatives are themselves concepts. One concept – to 'lengthen my arm' – can be carried out by 'using a stick'. Another concept alternative – to 'have the object travel to the ceiling by itself' – can be carried out by attaching the object to a ball and throwing it up to the ceiling.

So, in this example, we go from an idea (a ladder) to a concept, which becomes a fixed point for other ideas. But we also go from the concept itself to a 'broader concept', which becomes a fixed point for alternative concepts. Each of these alternative concepts becomes a fixed point for alternative ideas. So the two layers of concepts are used to cascade alternative ideas.

This is the 'concept fan'. At one end of the concept fan we have the purpose or objective of the thinking. How do we achieve the task? How do we get where we want to go? We work backwards. What broad concepts would move us towards this purpose? At the next level, what specific concepts would serve the broad concepts? Finally, what practical ideas could be used to deliver the concepts? This gives a cascade effect, with each level multiplying alternatives to the level below. It is a powerful way of generating alternatives to achieve a purpose.

For an alternative example, take a piece of paper and a pen. You start with the defined purpose of what you are trying to achieve at the right-hand side of the page. **For example, you might set out 'traffic congestion in cities'.** The implied purpose is how to deal with the problem of traffic congestion in cities. In your diagram, everything will need to flow or cascade from this point on the paper.

The next level lays out the broad concepts, or 'thinking directions', which might help tackle the problem. These might be: reduce traffic; improve traffic flow; increase travel space.

We then move backwards (towards the right-hand side of the page) to list the more specific concepts that could operate the broad concepts.

- For 'reducing traffic' we might have: restrict the number of vehicles; discourage traffic; reduce the need to travel; multi-user vehicles.
- For 'improving traffic flow' we might have: deal with peak travel problem at beginning and end of the day; remove junctions.
- For 'increasing travel space' we might have: more roads; smaller vehicles.

We then take each of the specific concepts and see how this could be put into action with specific ideas.

- For 'restricting the number of vehicles' we might have: high entry tolls; vehicle purchase permission auction (as in Singapore); special city access licences.
- For 'discouraging traffic' we might have: high congestion charges for entering the city (as in London); no provision for parking; poor-quality roads; publicise poor traffic flow.

- For 'reducing the need to travel' we might have: decentralise stores and offices; work from home via Internet, etc.; work stations.
- For 'multi-use transport' we might have: buses; trams; light rail; taxis; multi-user taxis.

The next broad concept was 'increasing traffic flow' and the concepts serving this could be delivered as follows:

- For 'remove peak traffic flow' we might have: staggered working hours; differential tolls; tax incentives.
- For 'remove junctions' we might have: overpasses and underpasses; roundabouts; a spiral road layout.

The next broad concept was 'increasing travel space' and the concepts could be delivered as follows:

- For 'more roads' we could have: underground roads; elevated roads; using riverbanks.
- For 'smaller vehicles' we could have: bicycles; lightweight motorcycles; very small cars, etc.

In this cascade effect, each point multiplies down to several points at the next level. It is very important to keep the 'broad concepts' (directions) as broad as possible. Too often people put specific concepts as broad concepts. These do not have the same multiplying effect.

Occasionally, it is useful to have yet another layer where the idea is made even more specific (where do we place the overhead road?)

The Concept Fan can be done by an individual or by a group working together. It is a way of generating alternatives through working downwards from very broad concepts.

PROVOCATION

There is a mathematical need for provocation in any self-organising system, otherwise the system gets stuck in a local equilibrium.

Traditional thinking makes much use of judgement. With judgement you come to an idea and then you judge it. You accept the idea or you reject it. For most parts of our life judgement is essential and extremely useful. The judgement of recognition allows us to make rapid use of past experience and also the experience of others. The judgement of assessment prevents us from making mistakes. Without judgement, it would be difficult to exist. So it is hardly surprising that the brain is a judgement machine. Nor is it surprising that philosophers have put all the emphasis on truth or judgement.

All that is very well, but lateral thinking requires a different operation. Instead of accepting or rejecting an idea you look at the idea in order to 'see where you can move to'. This puts a very different sort of usefulness on ideas.

One of the techniques of lateral thinking is to set up provocations.

Einstein used to carry out what he called 'thought experiments'. He would say, 'What would I see if I were travelling at the speed of light?' The child who places one block on top of the other 'to see what happens' is also carrying out an experiment.

Provocation has everything to do with experiments in the mind. Provocation allows us to make a statement that does not make sense, may contradict experience and may be totally illogical. We preface this with the signal word 'po', which indicates a provocation. 'Po' could be taken as implying a (P)rovocative (O)peration. It is also related to possible, hypothesis, pose, potential, etc.

Instead of just sitting and waiting for ideas, provocation provides a means by which you can unsettle your mind in order to increase the chance of having a new idea.

Using this, we create a provocation that lies outside our normal experience. This then provides a stepping stone which we can use to get across to the separate track – to point C. This was the idea of the factory being downstream of itself in Chapter 1.

Provocation and movement

We then use a new mental operation called 'movement' to move forward from the provocation to a new idea (the most extreme form of movement). So this is another way of moving laterally.

The general sense of 'movement' means the willingness to move forwards in a positive exploring way rather than stopping to judge whether something is right or wrong. We can use movement to move forwards from a weak idea to a stronger one. We can use movement to move forwards from a suggestion to a concrete idea. We can use movement to move forwards from a concept to an idea.

There are many ways of carrying out movement:

- You can extract a concept and then work with this.
- You can focus on the difference between the provocation and the usual situation.
- You can pick out the positive aspects and work with these.
- You can imagine the provocation put into action and see what happens.

Po, cars should have square wheels. This would be totally unacceptable to an engineer. You would need too much energy. The car would shake to pieces. The ride would be very bumpy. With 'movement', we imagine the square wheel rolling. It rises up on a point and then descends to a flat area. This is cyclical and is known in advance. So if the suspension was adapted in advance, you could get a smooth ride. From this, we develop the idea of 'anticipatory suspension'. A small jockey wheel in front of the car senses the bumpiness of the ground. This is signalled back so that the suspension reacts in advance. The wheel follows the contour of the ground, but the vehicle proceeds smoothly. If you run over bumpy ground, you do not bump up and down. The car remains steady but the wheels follow the profile of the ground. This idea was tried out by a motor manufacturer, who reported that it worked exactly as predicted. They did not use a jockey wheel but used pressure changes in the suspension itself. But the provocation had led to the development of a new suspension system.

Po, planes land upside down. This sounds totally absurd. If planes landed upside down, the wings would give a downward thrust. From this comes the idea of having two small winglets on normal planes. These would provide a 'negative bias', a downward thrust. If extra lift was needed in an emergency, these winglets would be cancelled – by folding them upwards, for example. This would instantly provide extra lift. Many plane accidents are caused by the inability to switch on extra lift immediately in an emergency situation. I discussed this idea at one point with some Boeing executives. Using provocation led to an interesting idea.

The logic of provocation

Mathematicians fully understand the need for provocation. Self-organising systems tend to settle down in a stable equilibrium, which is called a local equilibrium. They remain in that state until provocation moves them towards a more global equilibrium.

Mathematicians call the process 'annealing', which comes from making steel. The steel crystals lock into a position that is stable but not very strong. So you provoke them with heat again and they lock into a stronger position – and so on.

In a way, the mind also settles into a stable local equilibrium. Provocation is needed to move it into a more global equilibrium.

Ways of setting up provocations

The most important point to keep in mind is that a provocation is not a half idea or on the way to a possible idea. A provocation is related to the existing situation. Once you have the provocation, then you use it for its movement value.

Anything can be treated as a provocation. You can dismiss an idea in judgement terms and then choose to use that idea as a provocation. There are also formal ways of setting up provocations: escape, reversal, distortion, exaggeration and wishful thinking.

Arising

A remark that arises in the course of a discussion or a brainstorming session can be deliberately used as a provocation. This is not instead of judgement of that remark but in addition to judgement. You state that you are going to set up this provocation: 'Po . . .'

Escape

This is the easiest to use. We just pick something that we usually take for granted in a situation and we drop that thing or 'escape' from it. So, if we take for granted that watchdogs bark, we set up: 'Po, watchdogs do not bark.' From this develops the idea of training a dog to press with its paw a button that activates all alarm systems, alerts the police and sets off a tape recorder with a barking dog sound.

'Po, restaurants have no chairs.' Using 'moment to moment' movement we see people standing around and eating. They spend less time in the restaurant. From this comes the idea of charging by time as well as by the food eaten.

Reversal

Here we take a normal relationship and reverse it. Filters are there to remove some of the tar in cigarettes. 'Po, we add something instead of removing it.' What could we add? We could add air with a tiny pinhole so that, when you draw in smoke, you dilute it with air. This reduces the rate at which the harmful particles are deposited in the lungs (this is concentration related since it is an aerosol).

Distortion

Here there is a change in a sequence or a change in relationships. Normally, you pick up the phone, dial the number and speak. 'Po, you speak before you dial.' This can lead to two ideas. The first is voice-activated dialling – which exists. The second idea is to build a simple tape recorder into the phone. If you are using the phone to make a complaint or to order something, you can rehearse what you are going to say and say it into the recorder. Then you dial the number and, at the right moment, play the recording. This way you get your message right.

Exaggeration

This is an exaggeration, upwards or downwards of any dimension. It must be an actual dimension. 'Po, telephone calls can only last two minutes.' This suggests a compression technique so that you can talk at a normal speed, but the transmitted message is compressed so as to occupy less of the line time. The exaggeration must be unreasonable otherwise it has little provocative effect.

'Po, all voters have a hundred votes each.' This suggests that the votes are not just used at election time but can be used later to indicate approval or otherwise of the government. If the votes for the opposition reached a certain threshold, new elections would be called.

Wishful thinking

The provocation is in the form of 'wouldn't it be nice if . . .'. An example of this is the problem of the factory polluting the river.

So, we could also have a provocation 'Po, all telephone calls are friendly'. This suggests a green light on the phone. You would give an extra digit on your phone number but only to your friends. If one of them called, the green light would shine – but it wouldn't shine for other calls.

The provocation must be more than just a desire. It would not be very provocative to say 'Po, the trains were always on time'. But it would be provocative to say 'Po, you got paid for waiting for a train'.

Other provocations

The above ways of setting up provocations are not exhaustive. There are many other ways. What is important is that the provocation is meant to be a provocation. It is never meant to be an idea in itself. It is never meant to be just a desire for improvement.

The more unlikely a provocation seems, the more powerful it will be if you succeed in using that provocation. There is little value in weak or feeble provocations. They might seem easier to use but do not get you anywhere.

The head of a life assurance company in Canada set up the following provocation: 'Po, you die before you die.' As usual, this sounds totally impossible and illogical. From it, comes a powerful idea.

If the person insured gets a severe and probably terminal illness, the insurance company pays out 75 per cent of the death benefits. This provides money for hospital care and other expenses. The other 25 per cent of the benefits are paid on death. This has been widely taken up in North America, and is called 'Living Needs Benefits'. It has changed a concept that had been around for 123 years.

The person in question was Rob Barbaro, who subsequently became chief executive of Prudential Insurance (USA). This example shows that, even within traditional industry, it is possible to create a powerful new idea that opens up new opportunities. There was no need for Ron Barbaro to design a new idea. There was not a real problem to solve. But he is driven by creativity to develop new concepts and so open up opportunities.

MOVEMENT

Provocation is a basic way of getting movement. This does not exclude other techniques, all of which are discussed in more detail, for example, in my book *Serious Creativity*:

Extract the Concept: What concept do we see operating here? Can we extract this concept and seek to use it where we need the new idea? So you can ignore the rest of the provocation, and proceed with the rest of the idea you have 'extracted'.

Focus on the Difference: What are the points of difference between the provocation and the usual idea? Can we spell out, pursue and build on those points of difference? Even if the provocation appears to be very similar to the present way of doing things, can we make a conscious effort to explore that difference?

Positive Aspects: Are there any directly positive aspects of the provocation? What values are immediately present? Can we use these where we want the new idea? In other words, when a value is turned up by the provocation, we consider ways of achieving the value but in a more practical fashion.

Moment to Moment: We imagine the provocation put into action, even if this involves fantasy. We watch moment to moment. It is like watching a DVD frame by frame to watch what is going on. What do we see happening? From that we develop new ideas. This is how we work through the interesting concepts that come from 'Po, planes land upside down'.

Special Circumstances: Are there any special circumstances where the provocation would have direct value? The square wheels might have value if the ground was corrugated. Or 'Po, drinking glasses should have rounded bottoms' could have value if there were special holders for the glasses. Because everyone would need to use the special holders, polished furniture would not get white rings.

Movement remains a basic operation that can be used anywhere in creativity.

Random entry and movement

Let's say, with our original example, that when you leave home you always take the usual route into town. One day, on the outskirts of the town, your car breaks down and you have to walk home. You ask around for the best walking route and find yourself arriving home by a road you would never have taken on leaving home.

In a patterning system of thinking, if you start at the periphery and move towards the centre, you will arrive there by a route different from the one you might have taken if you had started at the centre. There is no mystery about it at all.

To use this random entry, you can never select the starting point, because any selection would relate to your current thinking. You have to use a random starting point. The simplest to use is a random word (nouns work best) – see Chapter 1 for the random word tool and exercise. You work backwards from this point and develop new ideas. This was the technique that generated 21,000 new ideas for a workshop in South Africa.

On a television programme in Holland, I was asked to use this technique there and then to generate new ideas for a sofa. By way of a random word the presenter opened a magazine. There was a picture of the Queen so I was given the random word 'queen'. Immediately my thoughts went to a queen-sized bed. From this came the idea of a large sofa with a rail running along each side. The back of the sofa could slide along these rails. If the back of the sofa was in the rear position, the sofa could be used as a bed. If the back was moved further forward, you could lounge and watch television. If the back was moved further forward still, you could sit and eat cucumber sandwiches. That is a new design for a sofa, and the whole process took 10 seconds from a random starting point.

SUMMARY: THE FORMAL TOOLS OF LATERAL THINKING

So the reason why creativity (idea creativity) has remained a mystery, and the reason why we have never developed these practical and formal tools for generating ideas, is that the word games of philosophy could never understand the asymmetric patterning behaviour of a self-organising information system like the human brain. Whenever I am talking to mathematicians or physicists, they fully understand the process.

New ideas are an essential part of thinking in every culture. We need new ideas for problem solving, for design, for invention and for simplifying things. We need new ideas for conflict resolution and designing the way forward. Relying on chance for new ideas is not very effective and not a sensible policy at all.

To do all this, we need tools and a structure as a key. Now that I have provided such tools – which have been tested over many years – there is the need for the will to use them.

3 Judgement Not Design

You can analyse the past but you have to design the future.

The whole emphasis of our intellectual culture and education is on judgement and analysis. Design is almost totally neglected.

The reason for this is that the thinking of the GG3 (Socrates, Plato and Aristotle) was totally judgement-based. Furthermore, the Church at the Renaissance needed judgement but had absolutely no use for design.

If you are going to be an architect, a graphic designer or a clothes designer you may get some education in design – but not otherwise. Yet design is fundamental to the thinking of everyone.

Design is putting together what we have in order to deliver the values we want. Judgement seeks the truth and makes decisions based on the past. Design seeks value and designs for the future.

Nothing I write here is intended to attack or diminish

the importance of judgement. That would be absurd. What I am insisting upon is that we introduce more design into our thinking and our education.

Judgement is concerned with 'what is'. Design is concerned with 'what could be'.

JUDGEMENT AND RECOGNITION

A doctor is in his clinic. A child is brought in with a rash. The doctor thinks of possibilities: food allergy, sunburn, measles, scarlet fever. The doctor then takes the child's history from the mother and examines the child. The doctor may do some additional tests.

In the end, measles is diagnosed. As soon as the diagnosis is made, the doctor can explain the progression of the illness to the mother. The doctor knows the probable course of the illness and the possible complications. Above all, the doctor knows the standard treatment.

That is the model for 100 per cent of education and 95 per cent of daily thinking.

Analyse the situation. Identify standard elements. Apply the standard answers. Education and training is all about identifying the standard elements and knowing the standard answers.

With judgement you come to an idea and then you judge it. You accept the idea or you reject it. For most parts of our life, judgement is essential and extremely useful. The judgement of recognition allows us to make rapid use of past experience and also the experience of óthers. The judgement of assessment prevents us from making mistakes. Without judgement, it would be difficult to exist. So it is hardly surprising that we have put all the emphasis on truth and judgement.

Is there anything wrong with this model? No. On the contrary, it is very practical and effective. But it is not enough. Instead of accepting or rejecting an idea you look at the idea in order to 'see where you can move to'. This puts a very different sort of usefulness on ideas. We need much more emphasis on design – for everyone.

THE DOG EXERCISE MACHINE

In an education magazine, I used to carry out a series of design exercises for children from the ages of four to 16. I would set a task and ask them to make a drawing showing how the task could be achieved.

Drawing is much more powerful than writing. Many youngsters would show complex negative feedback systems they could never have described in words. With drawings you can see the whole process at once. You can put your finger on a spot and ask, 'How does this happen?'

One of the design exercises was to design a dog exercising machine.

There were many ingenious designs. Most of them had a sort of treadmill with a bone suspended at one end. The dog ran on the treadmill to get the bone.

One youngster, aged five, had a different idea. His dog was towing a small trolley on which there was a car battery. An electrified prong came out of the battery. If the dog stopped, the trolley would run into it and the electrified prong would get the dog going again.

Almost everyone else was trying to get the dog to exercise, to move. This youngster was trying to prevent the dog from stopping. These designs were published as a book, *The Dog Exercising Machine*. There was also another collection published, with the title *Children Solve Problems*. The children weren't being led by what they knew – they were more creative in their approach to a problem. Using drawings helped.

OPERACY

Unfortunately, kids don't remain that creative for long.

Schools are involved with literacy and numeracy. They should also be involved with 'operacy', which is the skill of operating, or getting things done. In the real world, after leaving school, that is almost as important as literacy and numeracy.

For many years I was president of the Young Enterprise organisation. This involves thousands of youngsters in

Europe, Russia and some other countries setting up their own mini-businesses. They come up with a business concept, they devise the marketing and sales strategies and ultimately they learn the skills needed to operate a business. Some of them are very ingenious. Some of them are very successful. It is a wonderful concept.

For traditional reasons, based in the early medieval times, education has tended to look down on business as money-grabbing, commercial and not concerned with the higher things in life. In those days the upper classes were not interested in business, because their serfs and tenants provided the money and labour. This is an absurd attitude in today's world.

In the United Kingdom today, youngsters still leave school knowing the names of Henry Vlll's wives and even the date of the Treaty of Utrecht. At the same time they have no idea how the corner shop works or how the world of commerce operates.

Design and operacy

Every successful business started as a design in someone's mind. In general use, the word 'design' has an element of visual design and graphic design. Sometimes design is seen as a sort of cosmetic luxury. We badly need to broaden the meaning of the word 'design' to cover all those situations where we put things together to achieve some effect. Whenever standard routine is not enough, we need 'design'.

Operacy is about action and the skill of thinking for action instead of thinking for description. Design is part of operacy. Like action, design always has a purpose. With action we set out to achieve something. With design we set out to achieve something. Design is the basis for action.

DESIGN AND CONFLICTS

In conflicts, we seek to identify 'the bad guys' and to condemn them for bad behaviour or for breaking some law. Naturally, we seek to punish them. This may involve sanctions, fights, war, and so on.

The design approach is different and looks at the fears, needs and greed of those involved – on both sides.

In a conflict, the leaders on both sides derive their significance and importance from the continuation of the conflict. They have no real interest in solving the conflict because they will then lose any importance. If these leaders can be given a permanent position of importance that does not depend on the conflict, then the conflict will end.

I suggested this many years ago for the conflict in Northern Ireland. The conflict is now over.

A designed way forward for the Israel/Palestine conflict is to let each side vote in the elections of the other side. This need not be a full vote; it could be a half-vote. There would then be a good possibility of constructive politicians getting elected. Hardliners would have a much reduced chance of election. With constructive politicians on each side, the way forward would be more positive.

This design has a purpose, an aim to achieve something.

The court of design

Courts of law are always about judgement. Someone is guilty or innocent. Some party has done wrong to another party. They don't look at sorting out a way forward for the future. I once suggested to the top lawyer in the European Union the need for a court of design.

There are many matters that go to court that involve disputes between parties. This type of dispute can often be solved by using design. ADR (Alternative Dispute Resolution) and sometimes family courts adopt this approach. Sir Lawrence Street, in Australia, who is interested in my work, runs a successful design process for people with disputes.

Anyone could set up a court of design. It does not need to have official, government or legal standing. It just needs the people coming to this court to agree to take part in the process. They do not even need to agree to be bound by the outcome (this is not arbitration). This court, with staff skilled in creative design, will help them construct a way forward.

4 Knowledge and Information

Which is the more important on its own: a detailed road map or the ability to drive a car? Education is all about knowledge and information. This is necessary to fill the many hours devoted to education. How else would you fill these 'baby-sitting' hours?

Nothing I am writing here seeks to diminish the importance of information. Thinking without information is a self-indulgent game similar to those some philosophers play. What I am commenting upon is the notion that information is enough, that information is all. As with many other things I mention in the book, information is excellent – but it is not enough.

CHINA

Two thousand years ago, China was far ahead of the rest of the world in science and technology. They had gunpowder, printing, paper and the compass. Had China continued at the same rate of development, it would today be the hugely dominant country in the world in all respects: technically, scientifically and economically. So what went wrong? What brought the progress to a dead halt?

Scholars were a very important part of Chinese culture. They had a central position. One theory holds that the scholars decided that you could move from fact to fact to fact. As a result, they never developed the 'possibility system'. They never developed speculation, hypothesis and possibility. So progress came to an end, because without possibility you cannot progress.

Today the Chinese government is doing pilot projects with my school work in five provinces. If they like the results, it may be put into millions of schools.

COMPUTERS

The development of computers, with their superb ability to handle information, has made matters worse.

What happens when very young children are given computers? They develop the habit of searching for the answer they need. They no longer have to think – they just search for the answer. While the ability to search on a computer is excellent, the ability to think is also important.

The development of the Internet has allowed the organisation of a communal brain where lots of people apply their thinking to an issue. Unfortunately, a thousand poor thinkers does not itself give you good thinking. I know; I have tried it. The method is useful to sample what people are thinking but does not itself produce great thinking.

What about computers doing the thinking themselves? This is a possibility I would not rule out. They can already do some excellent thinking: analysis, extracting patterns and applying judgement. It is said that computer diagnosis of medical conditions is better than that of 90 per cent of doctors – providing the right information is fed into the computer.

So computers per se are not the problem. The main problem is perception, which I shall deal with later in this book. If computers have to work with our packaged perceptions, then they will not do better than us. If we can design computers to do their own perceiving, not guided by our frameworks, then computers will really think. That will be a good thing.

CORPORATIONS

What happened to China is happening today to major corporations. The excellence of our computers allows corporations to feed all the necessary data into a computer.

The computer analyses the data, and this analysis forms the basis for all decisions and strategy.

This is very, very dangerous. Because unless you make the effort to look at the data in different ways, you stagnate in the old concepts. I have seen that happen to many major corporations.

ALTERNATIVES AND POSSIBILITIES

As with China, the traditional logic habits within our education system do not put much emphasis on possibility – for obvious reasons. Possibilities are a very important part of thinking, but we regard them only as a way of getting to the truth. I have been at some of the most prestigious universities in the world: Oxford, Cambridge, London and Harvard. At none of them was any significant amount of time spent on possibilities and speculation. There is a brief acknowledgement that the 'hypothesis' is important in science – but that is all.

Possibilities and science

There is a very close link between possibilities and creativity because it is creativity that produces the possibilities. Almost every advance in science has depended on a creative possibility or hypothesis. Someone has often seen a possible alternative leading to an advance within the scientific field.

Peptic ulcer (stomach ulcer or duodenal ulcer) is a serious and widespread medical condition. In the past, people with this condition might have spent 20 years or more on antacids (to counter the acid in the stomach). They were supposed to avoid alcohol and spicy foods. Their life was a misery.

One day in the early 1980s, a young doctor in Western Australia named Barry J. Marshall and his colleague Robin Warren thought of the possibility that a peptic ulcer was an infection rather than a permanent condition. As an infection it could therefore be treated. Everyone roared with laughter. How could any bacteria survive the strong acid in the stomach? To prove his point, Marshall made a culture of the bug he suspected, drank it and gave himself an ulcer. Point proved.

Today, instead of spending 20 years or more on antacids, you just take antibiotics for a week and you are cured. Marshall and Warren won the Nobel prize in Physiology or Medicine in 2005 – they deserved it.

I was once taken out into the Arizona desert and shown some tall pillar-like cacti. I asked why cacti had spikes on them. That was apparently a silly question. Everyone knew that cacti had spikes on them to prevent animals from eating them. I observed that there were many parts of the world that had both plants and animals to eat them – so why did those plants not have spikes?

I suggested that there was a possibility that the small spikes on the cacti had nothing to do with animals. Those small spikes kept the boundary layer of air next to the plant stationary. That way the plant lost less water through transpiration and evaporation. I happened to tell someone my idea. He told me that the Israeli government were doing research on exactly this point – they were looking at how to grow plants with spikes so that they could survive in the desert.

Because action requires truth and certainty, we greatly underestimate the importance of possibilities. Most great advances in science are based on possibilities.

Research shows that people who smoke a lot of cannabis have an increased chance of developing schizophrenia. This may be so. But if we look at this information in a different way there is a possibility that people with a schizophrenic tendency enjoy cannabis more, and so more people with this tendency smoke cannabis heavily.

I once commented that I did not think that the Harvard Case Study method was a good way of teaching. Someone pointed out that a lot of brilliant people came out of the Harvard Business School. I pointed out that if a lot of brilliant people make their way towards an archway, then a lot of brilliant people will emerge from that archway. The archway has contributed very little. To get into Harvard you have to be brilliant, so when you come out you are still brilliant. There is a very real need to look at the information and data in new and different ways.

Possibilities and creativity

As we've seen, one of the formal tools of lateral thinking is 'challenge'. We need to use this to open up possibilities even when we are sure we have the right, and only, answer.

In traditional thinking, if there is an obvious and apparently satisfactory answer we stick with it and never explore other possibilities. We use possibilities only as a way of getting to the truth. If we believe we have already got to the truth, we do not need possibilities. One of the very important roles of creativity is to seek to look at data in different ways. Otherwise we remain stuck in old concepts, which the data can be used to support. Simply analysing data will not produce new ideas. If you want a really new idea you have to be able to start it off in your head, with creativity, and then check the idea out against the available data.

I have mentioned it before, but it is important enough to mention again. Once we have found the 'right answer' and the 'truth' we stop thinking. What is the point of thinking further?

The result is that there are many excellent ideas that completely block further progress. We do not think about these matters. There is the dangerous habit in psychology (especially in the USA) of calling all thinking 'problem solving'. So, if we do not perceive a problem, there is no point thinking about it.

I would say that this may be the most serious barrier to human progress.

Religion – truth or heresy?

Religion needs certainty and truth. It would be hard to be a martyr for possibility. Galileo got into trouble when his 'possibilities' challenged the certainty of the Church.

The Church needed the logic and certainty of the GG3 in order to prove heretics wrong. The Church could never accept heresies as possibilities.

While logic, truth and certainty (with the possibilities of hypotheses) have been very powerful in science, they have been limiting and even dangerous in other areas. Other people have other truths.

In perception, possibility is central. Do you look at a situation this way – or that way? You always need to keep possibilities in mind.

If we really want truth, why should we bother with possibilities? There are a number of reasons:

- There is the obvious need for possibility as a hypothesis or framework on the way to finding the truth.
- Truths accepted too easily can be challenged by opening up alternative possibilities (as suggested above).
- There are times when you have to live with many possibilities as you cannot determine the truth. This is often the case with perception.

The pre-Socratic philosophers in ancient Greece had much more to say about 'possibility' and invented the hypothesis. For obvious reasons the Church preferred the logic and truth of the GG3.

Creative possibilities

There is a type of examination called 'multiple choice'. The candidate is asked a question and then given a list of possible answers. The candidate then chooses their answer from this list.

The advantages of this system are obvious in terms of marking the papers. Has the right answer been chosen or not? Papers can be marked mechanically by computer. This is much more fair than the subjective judgement of an essay.

Research has shown, however, that creative students get marked down with such a system. The less-creative student chooses answer 'C' and cannot see the possibility of any other answer. The creative student can see that under certain circumstances the answer could be 'D'. In choosing 'D', or even in spending extra time deciding between possibilities, the creative student is going to do less well than the uncreative one.

Exactly the same thing applies to IQ tests. At the beginning, IQ tests were used to see how a child compared with others from better backgrounds, so the 'right' answer was the one given by the others. So if a child was different and saw different possibilities, they were marked down.

You may be expected to choose a certain word, but a creative person can see the possibility of a different word.

In a court of law the creative lawyer can show a possible alternative explanation for the evidence. This creates a 'reasonable doubt', and in a criminal case the accused has to be acquitted.

Possibility is at the heart of creativity. We need to know how to handle possibility in a practical way. Without possibility creativity is impossible.

The tennis tournament

There is a singles tennis tournament. It is a knockout tournament. One player plays against another and the winner plays the winner of another match – and so on until there is a final winner. There is one final, two semi-finals, four quarter-finals, and so on. On this occasion there are 72 entries. How many games will be required to find the winner?

I sometimes use this problem in my seminars. It is not difficult to work out in the traditional way, but the audience usually get quite upset when I only give them 10 seconds to find the answer.

With this problem, we normally seek to find the winner. With lateral thinking, there is another possibility. Forget about producing a winner; let us find the losers. With 72 entrants there will be 71 losers. Each loser is produced by one game. So 71 games are needed. That only takes five seconds.

Another task is to add up the numbers from one to 10. This task is not difficult and you should get the answer

55. Now add up the numbers from one to 100. Again the task is not difficult, but it will take time and you might make a mistake.

Instead, imagine the numbers from one to 100 written down in a row as suggested below:

$$1 \quad 2 \quad 3 \quad \ldots \quad 98 \quad 99 \quad 100$$

Then repeat the numbers from one to 100, but write them backwards under the first set of numbers as shown:

$$
\begin{array}{ccccccc}
1 & 2 & 3 & \ldots & 98 & 99 & 100 \\
100 & 99 & 98 & \ldots & 3 & 2 & 1
\end{array}
$$

If you add up each pair of numbers, you will always get 101 because, as you go along, the top number increases by one and the bottom number decreases by one. The total number must stay the same. So the total is 100 x 101, or 10100.

This is, of course, twice the total we needed because we wrote down two sets of numbers from one to 100. So we divide the total by two and get 50 x 101, or 5050.

Another approach might be to 'fold' the numbers over on themselves to give:

$$
\begin{array}{ccccccc}
1 & 2 & 3 & \ldots & 48 & 49 & 50 \\
100 & 99 & 98 & \ldots & 53 & 52 & 51
\end{array}
$$

Again the total of each pair is 101. This gives 50 x 101, or 5050.

This method is not only very quick, but there is little chance of making an error. In short, it is a much faster and much better way of coming to the correct answer.

Danger of possibility

Beware. Some information together with a possibility can quickly condense into a certainty. Consider what happened with vampires.

A certain Elizabeth Bartolo was told that if she had a bath in the blood of virgins she would live for ever. So she had her servants find virgins and exsanguinate them. They then dumped the bloodless bodies around the area. What was the possibility?

There is a blood disease called porphyria which has several effects. One of them is severe skin rashes caused by exposure to sunlight. So such people stayed indoors and only appeared in the evening. Their skin was unusually white as a result. Another effect of porphyria is bleeding gums. So white-faced people with bleeding gums only appeared during the evening or night.

Then there were the bloodless corpses found around the area. The result was a belief in vampires.

Vampires were supposed to be allergic to garlic. By chance, two people I know with porphyria are also allergic to garlic! A possibility becomes more and more certain.

Possibilities with a good story can quickly become fact and belief. So we are right to be wary of possibility. At the same time we have to accept the huge importance of possibility in thinking.

It took me about 20 years to find a way of attaching my napkin so that my tie was not dirtied during a meal. I tried all sorts of clips and pins but invariably lost them by leaving them on the table. The final solution is incredibly simple. If I remember to describe it later in this book, you can use it immediately instead of waiting 20 years like I had to. That is the power of knowledge. So knowledge is essential – but so are possibilities.

ARGUMENT

If you have invented logic, there is much more fun in showing someone to be wrong than in proving a point. Those who do not yet understand logic will not appreciate your proof but they will appreciate your attack. Furthermore, as you seek to teach your logic to others, you will spend most of the time pointing out their errors.

So argument was invented, perfected and disseminated by the GG3. Socrates in particular was very interested in dialectic or argument.

Argument became such a central method that, amazingly, we have been content to use it for 2,400 years in all sorts of areas. We use it in parliament and in government. We use it in the courts of law. We use it in business negotiations. We use it in family disagreements and discussions. It works very well. There was, and is, a real need for a method of showing incorrect ideas and positions to be wrong. Without that there would be chaos.

Yet it is a crude, primitive and very inefficient way of exploring ideas. Argument works best when we are seeking to destroy a position, statement or assumption. It works well when we are trying to decide between two different positions.

Argument does not work well at all when we are seeking to explore a subject. It is negative. It has no generative qualities. Argument is a very good way of establishing the truth but useless for exploration. Exploration means exploring and discovering new aspects of the subject. Argument can only be concerned with 'know' aspects. You can argue about which road to take on a road map, but argument cannot create the road map.

Unfortunately, we use argument to explore a subject because we have no alternative method.

Faults of argument

The following faults of argument apply to the use of argument to explore a subject:

- Argument is destructive and negative and concerned with attack.
- There is no design element. There is no attempt to design a way forward. It is win or lose.

- If 5 per cent of the other position is wrong, then the whole time is spent on this 5 per cent.
- A weak idea that cannot be attacked will prevail against a stronger but more vulnerable idea.
- There is a huge temptation to show off your superiority by proving the other party wrong – even on trivial points.
- There is too much ego play.
- A person who is skilled at argument may win against a less skilled person even if this other person has a better case.
- There is no generative energy or skill to develop new positions.

It is only fair to say that argument was never designed to explore a subject.

ALTERNATIVES TO ARGUMENT

Is there any alternative to argument for exploring a subject? There is now – for the first time in 2,400 years – one example of which is given in the next section.

Why has it taken so long to come up with such a simple and powerful method? Because our intellectual culture and education was determined by the Church in the Middle Ages and argument was what the Church needed to prove heretics wrong.

Parallel thinking

Imagine a rather ornate building of a square shape. There are four people, each of whom is facing one aspect of this building. Through a mobile phone or walkie-talkie, each person is insisting and arguing that he or she is facing the most beautiful aspect of the building.

Parallel thinking means that they change how they go about this argument. All four people move around to the south side of the building together. Then all of them move on to the west side. Then the north and finally the east side. So all of them, in parallel, are looking at the same side of the building at any one moment.

Instead of argument, where A is adversarially attacking B, we have a system where A and B are both looking and thinking in the same direction – but the directions change as they move around. That is parallel thinking.

In our lives we need a symbol to indicate the direction of thinking at any one moment to ensure we are thinking in the same direction.

A zebra is grazing and hears a rustle in the grass. A chemical is released in the brain, which sensitises all the circuits concerned with danger. As soon as the lion appears, the zebra is prepared to flee. The reverse happens in the lion's brain. As soon as the lion sees the zebra, the chemicals alert the lion's brain to positive action.

For such reasons we need to separate out the modes of thinking because there is confusion if we try and do everything at once. We end up just operating in a negative mode.

The purpose of the Six Hats is to separate the modes of thinking and to ensure that everyone is thinking in parallel in the same mode at any one moment. We use the symbol of the Thinking Hat.

The Six Thinking Hats

I designed this method in 1984. It is now very widely used by four-year-olds in school and by top executives in the world's largest corporations.

- ABB in Finland used to take 30 days for their multinational project discussions. Using the Six Hats, they do it in two days.
- Siemens told me they had reduced their product development time by 50 per cent through using the Six Hats.
- Someone at IBM told me that at their top laboratory, meeting times had been reduced to one-quarter of their original duration.
- J.P. Morgan in Europe reduced meeting times to one tenth.
- When the Boxing Day tsunami hit Sri Lanka in 2004, the various aid agencies seemed unable to plan a way forward. The Sri Lankan government invited my trainer, Peter Low, over from Singapore. In two days they had agreed a plan of action. The Sri Lankan government now insists that all aid agencies learn the Six Hats method.

- Grant Todd in the USA did research on the use of the Six Hats in jury discussions. Juries reached unanimous decisions very rapidly. Judges were so impressed that in some states the judge can recommend that the jury learn the system. This may be the first change in the jury system for over 1,000 years.
- MDC in Canada did a careful costing and found that they saved $20 million in the first year of using the Six Hats.
- Statoil in Norway had a problem with an oil rig that was costing them $100,000 a day until they fixed it. They had been thinking about it for some time. Then Jens Arup, one of my trainers, introduced the Six Hats. In 12 minutes they had solved the problem and saved $10 million.

The hats

There is no fixed order of use. You can choose the sequence you want. In training, some of the more useful sequences will be suggested.

Blue Hat: This is the organising or control hat. It is rather like the conductor of an orchestra. It is used right at the beginning of a discussion to decide the focus and what sequence of hats to use. During the meeting the chairperson or facilitator metaphorically wears the Blue Hat in a disciplinary way. People are reminded of the hat in use if they stray from that mode. The Blue Hat is used at

the end for the outcome, summary and next steps. The
Blue Hat is like a bookend: one at the beginning and one
at the end.

White Hat: Think of white and paper and printout. The
White Hat is concerned with information. What information do we have? What information is missing? What
information do we need – and how are we going to get
it? Questions can be asked under the White Hat. If con-
flicting information is put forward, there is no argument.
Both versions are put down in parallel and then discussed
when that information needs to be used.

Red Hat: Think of red and fire and warmth. The Red Hat
is to do with feelings, emotions, intuition. Under the Red
Hat all participants are invited to put forward their
feelings. In a normal discussion you can only put forward
these things if they are disguised as logic. Here there is no
need to justify or explain them. They exist and can
therefore be put forward. The Red Hat period is very brief
and simply allows these things to be put forward.

Black Hat: Think of the black of a judge's robes. The
Black Hat is for critical thinking. What is wrong with
the idea? What are its weaknesses? The Black Hat looks
at the down side, why something will not work, the risks
and dangers. All the negative comments that might be
made during a meeting are concentrated under the Black

Hat. The Black Hat is very useful, possibly the most useful of all the hats, but it has its defined place.

Yellow Hat: Think of sunshine and optimism, dawn and a new day. This focuses on the positive. What are the benefits? The values? How could it be done? Education is mostly about critical thinking. We never really develop 'value sensitivity'. This means the ability to find value in anything – even things we do not like and will not use. Nevertheless we should, honestly and objectively, find value in such things. Without value sensitivity, creativity can be a waste of time. I have sat in on meetings where good ideas have been generated but no one has been able to see the value of the ideas.

Green Hat: Think of vegetation, growth and branches. This is directly concerned with creativity. When the Green Hat is in use, participants are expected to make a creative effort or keep quiet. They do not like keeping quiet so they make that effort. This means looking for new ideas. It means considering alternatives, both the obvious ones and new ones. It means generating possibilities. It means modifying and changing a suggested idea, possibly through the deliberate use of lateral thinking tools.

That is all there is. Six Hats that allow us to think in parallel to explore a subject in a constructive and not adversarial way. This Six Hats method of parallel thinking challenges all those at the meeting to use their minds fully and not just in the adversarial mode. Someone who is against the idea being discussed is expected honestly and objectively to be able to see the values in the idea.

The framework of the Six Hats might seem at first to complicate discussions and make them much longer. In fact, use of the Hats reduces meeting time to a quarter or even a tenth. Proper training in the method is recommended, but years of experience across a wide range of cultures, levels and sectors have shown that it works very well.

Showing off

One of the attractions of argument is that you can show your superiority by proving someone else wrong. You cannot do that with the Six Hats. If you want to show off, you can only do it by performing better under each hat.

Under the White Hat you think of more information or better questions than anyone else. Under the Black Hat you think of more dangers and risks. Under the Yellow Hat you show more values. Under the Green Hat you put forward more ideas and possibilities.

This is the showing off of performance – not of attack.

EXCELLENT – BUT NOT ENOUGH

As with so many other concepts in this book, I want to make it clear that argument is an excellent method when used in the right place. But it is not enough. We need a different method and framework (software) for exploring a subject in a constructive way.

The US Air Force once published research on team performance. They compared teams put together according to psychological profiles and tests, and teams put together simply on a preference for one of the Six Hats. On every score the Six Hats teams performed better than the others. This may be due to what is known as cognitive dissonance (having made a choice, you live up to it).

SUMMARY: KNOWLEDGE AND INFORMATION

Last year I was told by a Nobel prize economist that he had been at the economics meeting in Washington the previous week, and they had been using the Six Hats. Later in the year, a woman in New Zealand told me she had been teaching the Six Hats in the highlands of Papua New Guinea (often regarded as the most primitive place on Earth). She went back a month later and they told her it had changed their lives.

It is an extremely simple method, but very powerful. Why did it take 2,400 years to develop? Because we were so happy with the excellence of argument!

5   Language

Language is an encyclopaedia of ignorance. A word enters a language and then becomes fixed. The word may have entered the language a long time ago at a time of relative ignorance. Once the word exists, it affects our perception and we are forced to see the world in that way.

If there is something very new and defined then we might create a new word, such as 'computer', but it is very difficult to change existing words to have a different meaning on purpose.

I introduced the term 'lateral thinking' in my first book *The Use of Lateral Thinking* in 1967 (the book was titled *New Think* in the USA). My interest in thinking had come from three sources. As a Rhodes scholar, I had studied psychology at Oxford and this gave me some interest in thinking. In the course of medical research I used computers extensively and I had become interested in the sort of thinking that computers could not do, which was creative and perceptual thinking. Continuing my medical research at Harvard, I had worked on the complicated way in which the body regulated blood pressure and the general integration of systems in the human body. This had led to an interest in self-organising systems.

These three strands (thinking, perceptual thinking and self-organising systems) had come together and I had already completed the manuscript of the book and called it *The Other Sort of Thinking*. Then, in an interview with a journalist, I said that, for thinking that was not linear, sequential and logical, 'You needed to move laterally instead of going straight ahead.' I realised the value of the term – it was the word I needed – and I put in into the book instead of the other phrase.

On a more technical level lateral thinking means moving 'laterally' across patterns rather than just moving along them. The term Lateral Thinking is now very widely in use and has its own entry in the Oxford English Dictionary.

It was necessary to create the term – 'lateral thinking' – for two reasons. There was a need to describe idea creativity and to distinguish it from artistic creativity. The word also indicates the logical basis for creativity by describing movement across asymmetric patterns in a self-organising information system (the human brain). On a more general level, 'lateral thinking' also implies that you cannot dig a hole in a different place just by digging the same hole deeper. It may be necessary to change the perceptions, concepts and approach rather than work harder with the existing perceptions, concepts and approach.

There was an absolute need to create the new word 'po'. This signals that a provocation is to follow. Saying things like: 'cars should have square wheels' or 'planes should land upside down' would make no sense at all unless they were seen as provocations (from which interesting ideas arise using the operation of 'movement'). Self-organising systems, like the brain, reach a stable state or a local equilibrium. Mathematicians know that provocation is needed in order to move towards a more global equilibrium. So there is an absolute need for a provocative operation in language. This did not exist, so it was necessary to create one.

JUDGEMENT AND BOXES

Language is a judgement system. Things we perceive are put into boxes with a label on them. We see something that we recognise or judge to be a car.

Immediately we see it as a car, the whole 'pattern' or file is opened and we have access to all we know about cars. The label or word is the connection between the external world and our stored knowledge. We probably could operate without words but it would be far less efficient.

The word 'is' indicates a definite judgement – not a

possibility. We do not have a practical word to indicate that something is possible. We really need a word to indicate that something is just possible or quite probable. We could do that with a whole sentence, as I have done here, or we could use the phrase 'may be'. A simple word would allow us to see the world in a more complex and subtle way.

We have a word for 'friend' and a word for 'enemy'. Some people can be fitted into one of those two boxes. We do not really have a neutral word for someone who is neither a friend nor an enemy but with whom we have to deal. We could use the word 'acquaintance', but you would not call your tax inspector or your car mechanic an acquaintance. We certainly do not have a word for someone who is half friend and half enemy (or different proportions). There are many people who are friends but who, under difficult circumstances, or when placed under pressure, can become enemies.

COMPLEX SITUATIONS

Language is even more inadequate when dealing with complex situations. Such situations can usually be described in a sentence or even a paragraph. Such descriptions may be adequate but they do not place that situation in our perception range – it is difficult to recognise such a situation without a single word.

Consider the following negotiating situation: 'Unless the benefits are laid out more clearly and unless you are prepared to give up on some of your fixed demands, we shall not make much progress. I would like you to lay out clearly what you see as the benefits for my side.'

Such a description may adequately describe the situation but is cumbersome and even awkward to use.

We do have a word like 'supermarket' to describe a quite complex operation in a succinct way. We do not, however, have a word for a conflict that cannot be solved because the leaders on each side do not want to solve the conflict (because they would instantly lose their importance).

There is an absolute need for a new sort of language that allows us to perceive, recognise and communicate complex situations instantly. Our actions and behaviour would be greatly improved. We would no longer be forced into the very limited boxes offered by traditional language.

LANGUAGE AND PERCEPTION

So, while language is immensely valuable for thinking, there is also a downside. Language freezes perceptions into concepts and words. These words then determine our perceptions for ever into the future. Think how, as I mentioned, the word 'enemy' determines our perception of someone with whom we disagree. We do not have a word that indicates someone who is half good and half bad. The crudeness of language has a negative effect on perception and then on thinking.

Some sort of 'coding' is inevitable in human progress. To overcome this language situation I have invented a coding system that allows us to describe complex situations instantly and launched it on the Internet. Of course, being a code, it cuts across all languages and can be used to communicate with someone speaking a different language.

Some of the codes are arbitrary fixed codes. For example, we might say, 'We have a code 53 here.' That conveys the whole meaning given above. Others can be constructed from a basic matrix of nine key concepts. (See www.debonocode.org for the codes.)

SUMMARY: LANGUAGE

Language is an extremely valuable device and we could never have progressed far without it. But language is by no means as perfect or as complete as we may believe. A lot of further development is needed and this will not happen by chance.

The code system mentioned above is necessary. Such a system also allows for international communication. You can use English to find the code but then people can understand your code in Chinese, Russian, German, Telugu or any language at all – provided there is a simple version of the code in that language.

6   Democracy

Winston Churchill once said: 'Democracy is the worst form of Government except all those other forms that have been tried from time to time.' Though democracy isn't perfect, it is better than all the other systems – such as dictatorship, tyranny, absolute monarchy, and so on.

OTHER AND PRECEDING SYSTEMS

The Phoenicians had a different system of government. There was an upper chamber made up of representatives of different sectors of society – merchants, farmers, priests, workers, etc. This was the governing chamber. If they agreed on something it became law. If there was disagreement in this chamber then the matter went to the second chamber, which was a people's assembly.

The Venetians had a complex but successful system that lasted for a thousand years. In it, people were elected to a chamber. Then a number of people were selected by lot (chance) to go to a second chamber. The same process was repeated in different stages until a government was formed. So there was the people element – they were voted in – but also the chance element, but from an enriched group. This method successfully prevented factions, party formation and corruption, which wrecked so many medieval republics.

Then there is the system with a monarch or sheikh and an assembly that can advise but does not have the final say.

ADVANTAGES OF DEMOCRACY

Democracy is a pretty good system. It is better for stability than for growth. The greatest advantage is that people cannot complain because they made the choice. Sometimes this is rather like a condemned man asked to choose the method of his execution. He makes the choice.

There is also always the possibility of change at the next election. Many dictators have been in power for over 40 years; politicians have to be careful not to upset the people or they will not be elected next time round. The press, on behalf of the people, are ready to criticise the government. Democracy prevents tyranny, mistakes, excesses. Democracy is good at preserving stability. People see that they have made a choice themselves and are prepared to live with this (provided elections are seen as fair).

LIMITATIONS OF DEMOCRACY

Democracy was designed to prevent tyranny, not to facilitate progress. The emphasis is on attack, criticism and argument rather than the generation of new possibilities. It is much easier to be attacked for doing something than for doing nothing (even if existing systems may be deteriorating), so very little gets done.

The talent and skill of the opposition is largely wasted while they are in opposition, where they are confined to attacking and being negative.

The sharp division of the population into parties can create tensions and violence, as happened in 2008 in both Kenya and Pakistan. One group is set against another. Each feels it will be disadvantaged if the other group is in power – which is sometimes the case.

Blocked by openness

You are driving down the road and you come to a police barrier. You cannot proceed further.

We all know about being blocked by a barrier or something in the way. But what about being blocked by openness? What about being blocked precisely because there is nothing in the way?

You proceed down the open and familiar highway. This very openness of the road prevents, or blocks, you from taking a side road.

There are concepts and ways of doing things that seem so excellent that we are prevented, or blocked, from seeking alternatives. Democracy as a form of government is one such example. Because it is rather better than other and preceding forms of government, we never think how it might be improved by creativity.

Change

Democracy is not beyond change, although any change will be strongly resisted by those who benefit from the present system and those who believe it is perfect. Below I make some suggestions. These are only possibilities.

A very simple change is to have parliament use the Six Hats framework – at least on one day a week. The Speaker would announce that it was Yellow Hat time, and members would be expected to make positive comments. At Black Hat time they would be permitted their usual criticisms. At Green Hat time there would be an opportunity for creativity, suggestions and modifications of ideas. At the end of the day there might be Red Hat time, when members could insult each other at will. I discussed this idea with the prime minister of Mauritius. He liked it and might try it some time.

Another suggestion is to create some new seats, equivalent in number to one-third of the seats in the parliament (this number is only a suggestion and might need to be reconsidered). There would be no one sitting in these seats. These seats would be counted as voted for by public opinion. If the opposition put forward an idea and a poll of public opinion was 70 per cent in favour of that idea, then 70 per cent of the seats would have voted for the idea. In this way there would be a continuous input from the public instead of having to wait for the next election. The opposition could also bring forward legislation instead of just being in a critical role. In this model, however, public opinion would only be one factor, and not the sole factor in deciding legislation.

Another possibility is to have a National Council for New Ideas. This council would generate and collect new ideas. These would be tested in public opinion polls, pilot schemes, surveys, etc. If everyone liked the ideas, then the government could choose to use the ideas – but would not be compelled to do so. The government could also use the council to try out its own ideas (kite-flying, i.e. making visible an idea to judge reaction to that idea). This way the government could get the benefit from successful ideas without having to take responsibility for unsuccessful ideas if the public rejected them. I have set up such a Council in Serbia. It is currently very difficult for a democratic government to try out ideas in this way.

Constructive thinking

Someone who is charismatic on television or in the media stands a good chance of getting elected in a democratic system. Most people in democratic politics also tend to be lawyers, journalists and teachers. This is because architects, engineers, business executives, entrepreneurs and scientists cannot risk entering politics. If they are elected, they have to give up their current job. These jobs are in hierarchy organisations and depend on continuing public visibility. If you step out of a job in these careers you cannot go back to the same position so, if they are not elected next time, they cannot go back to their old job. The risk is not worthwhile.

In their training, lawyers, journalists and teachers are good at talking and arguing; they are more used to criticising than to creative and constructive thinking. Since they outnumber more creative and constructive thinkers, this is a serious structural problem with democracy.

There is a great need for creativity to challenge ideas with which we are perfectly happy. Such ideas may be blocking the path to better ideas.

Perhaps there could be a way of allowing constructive people to participate in government without giving up their current job. Perhaps the endless debates in the legislative chamber are no longer so essential. Perhaps it could all be done by e-mail!

In today's age of new technologies, we do not have to be restricted to the methods available to the ancient

Greeks, who created democracy. There could even be an ongoing assessment of each member of parliament by their constituents, and their vote in the chamber would reflect this assessment. So if someone got a 50 per cent rating, he would have half a vote in the chamber. A 20 per cent rating would mean only a fifth of the vote. Technically this is possible today.

SUMMARY: DEMOCRACY

Creativity is not only involved in changing ideas and processes that are in use, such as democracy. Creativity can be involved in designing completely new things that take advantage of changes in technology, etc. With Facebook, YouTube, eBay, etc., the Internet has given some people the opportunity to design new programmes.

So creativity in design may involve getting rid of problems and inconveniences. Creativity in design may reduce price or increase longevity of the product.

And creativity in design may involve putting together familiar ingredients in a new way – just like creating a new dish from traditional ingredients.

Democracy is designed to keep society stable and to protect it from tyranny. It is not designed for progress. More thinking is needed.

7 Universities

As I mentioned before, I have been to a number of universities (Malta, Oxford, London, Cambridge, Harvard) as an undergraduate, a postgraduate and in a teaching post. I also have a collection of degrees (BSc, MD, MA, DPhil, PhD, DDes, LLD). Four of these were earned, and the others were *honoris causa.*

I have a great respect for universities, but the theme of much of this book applies to them as well: 'Excellent but not enough.' In other words, universities are excellent at the game they have come to play, but this game is not enough. Being blocked by excellence is always the danger.

TRUTH, KNOWLEDGE AND SCHOLARSHIP

An obsession with the truth can hardly be criticised as wrong. But this obsession can prevent development of the mentally important role of speculation and possibility. When the world was full of speculation and fantasy, this obsession with the truth served society very well. Today the world is not so full of fantasy, and attention to possibility has become rather more important.

The original purpose of universities was to bring the wisdom of ages and make it available to students of the present. That role of scholarship is still performed very well. It is, however, not enough.

When as an undergraduate I was reading psychology at Oxford, I found that it was all about the history of psychology. There was very little consideration of current concerns, speculations, problems or practical points. It was enough to know that someone had proposed an idea in 1850, and then in 1922 there was another theory, and so on.

At Harvard I was interested in the control of blood pressure in the human body. I found it more useful to discuss matters with the Professor of Aeronautics at the Massachusetts Institute of Technology (MIT), because he was interested in systems behaviour, whereas Harvard had this scholarship attitude to historic events and ideas.

I had had an operation and was unable to attend an international conference on thinking. So I had a long conversation on the telephone with a friend of mine, Professor David Perkins of Harvard University, and this was broadcast to the participants.

I remember his frequent emphasis on 'understanding'.

If we have knowledge we have understanding, and from that we can proceed to action. Of course, I agree with this. But understanding is not itself enough. We also need frameworks of possibility in order to make progress.

I admit that it is not easy to keep an ultimate concern with the truth and yet to open up creativity and possibility as well, but it is necessary.

THINKING

Because of the concern with the truth, universities have had to concentrate on critical thinking. Once again this is excellent but not enough. Creative thinking, design thinking and perceptual thinking should also be included.

Truth may prevent stupid and nasty things from happening, but truth in itself does not make things happen. For that we need design thinking.

I would suggest that every university course has a foundation year with two main subjects. The first of these would be thinking. This would include my thinking (practical creativity) and any other approach that is operational rather than descriptive.

The second subject would be the state of the world and society. It is not enough for anyone to know a particular subject in great depth while remaining ignorant of the world around them.

DESIGN

Analysis is wonderful but it is not enough. Knowledge and analysis may give us the road map but then we have to design our journey. Where do we want to go?

Design means putting together what we have in order to deliver the values we want. Design is all about the real world. Design is all about the world outside schools and universities. How do you design your career? How do you design your life? How do you design a car park? How do you design a political manifesto?

Right from the beginning, students should be set simple design exercises. These need not be relevant to the subjects they are studying. The purpose of these exercises is to develop the thinking skills of design. The exercises may include designing a bus; designing a holiday resort; designing a sport for old people; designing a café; designing a car park; designing a new type of examination.

Design brings in aspects of action, practicality and value.

You can analyse the past but you have to design the future – or else you will just fall into it.

THE SIX VALUE MEDALS

Universities and all educational institutions completely ignore value. It is assumed that everyone knows about current values and that this will therefore guide their thinking, behaviour and designs.

A very important operation is to be able to extract 'value' at every point. What is the value here? For whom is there a value?

The value may indeed be hidden in a lot of negatives, but you need to identify that value.

In the end creativity has to show value. Being different for the sake of being different is not creativity.

Values may seem intangible, but they do need more direct attention.

In my book *The Six Value Medals*, I look at six different types of value:

Gold Medal: Human values – the things that matter directly to people, both positive and negative: praise, achievement, humiliation, and so on.

Silver Medal: Organisational values – whether the organisation is a corporation or a family unit. This involves the purpose and mission of that organisation. How do the values help or impede that purpose?

Steel Medal: These are the quality values. Whatever something is supposed to be doing, how well is it being done? Steel has certain quality requirements.

Glass Medal: Glass is a simple substance, but with

creativity much can be done with it. So the Glass Medal is concerned with innovation and creativity. What is new?

Wood Medal: Ecology values. This is ecology in its broadest sense and not just nature. It includes the impact of any action on the world around.

Brass Medal: Brass looks like gold but is not. This medal is concerned with perceptual values. How will something be perceived? Something worthwhile might be perceived badly. Something less worthwhile might be perceived more favourably. We may wish it otherwise but we need to pay attention to perceptual values.

The book includes methods of carrying out and displaying the results of a 'value scan' so that people can compare their own subjective scans and focus on the points of disagreement.

Universities should look at teaching values.

It is also important to identify under what circumstances the values would be present. How durable would these values be?

In the end, 'value' is the currency of creativity. If creativity does not deliver value it is a pointless exercise.

ARGUMENT

Universities are much concerned with argument as a way of arriving at the truth. This goes back to medieval days, when verbal disputes were used especially in matters of theology.

While argument has a value, there is also a genuine need to understand the other point of view and to seek reconciliation. There is a need to design a way forward rather than just to win an argument. What are the values, perceptions and fears of the other party?

With theology, constructive thinking probably suggested compromise, but in other matters, constructive thinking is a powerful way forward.

EXAMINATIONS

I used to examine for the medical finals at Cambridge University. About 10 per cent of the candidates were so poor you wondered how they had ever got so far and whether they could ever become doctors. Eighty-five per cent were competent and grey. They had the right answers but nothing more. Only about 5 per cent showed some spark of originality or even thinking. Perhaps that is the nature of medicine as a subject – competence is all.

Examinations are good for testing whether someone knows what he or she is supposed to know. They are even more useful for getting people to study.

I asked students where they picked up their knowledge. They told me that seeing patients in a hospital ward was motivating but that very little could be learned because the variety of different cases was necessarily limited. They said they went to lectures to know the 'bandwidth' of the knowledge they were expected to have. They said they got almost all the required knowledge from books. So maybe the role of the university was just to recommend the right books.

Possibly, instead of formal exams there could be random micro-exams. A computer screen would ask for a particular student, who would be given simple questions to answer there and then. The results of these micro-exams would then be put together to create a final mark. This would test thinking and knowledge in a different way.

The game

Over time, and for good reasons, an academic 'game' has developed. You are supposed to play that game. A very eminent scientist once asked me why I did not have lists of references in my books. I replied that it was because the ideas were mine and not obtained through scholarly research into other people's work. He told me that nevertheless I should 'fake' a reference list, whether or not I had read the works, because this was what was expected – this was 'the academic game'.

SKILLS

I have mentioned earlier that the main role of universities in the future might be to teach skills. These skills might include:

Information skills: How to get needed information from various sources, including digital sources, books and university staff.

Thinking skills: How to think critically, creatively, constructively and in a design mode.

People skills: Dealing with people, managing people, understanding people.

Professional skills: Skills relating to the chosen profession.

SUMMARY: UNIVERSITIES

I was once invited to speak at the World University Presidents' Summit held in Bangkok. I told the audience that in a digital age, universities were out of date.

The original purpose of a university was to bring the knowledge and information of the past and make it available to the students of today. In a digital age it is possible to get all the information you want without going to university. With the development of a new profession of 'information provider', you will simply contract with the provider to get you the needed information. Today, universities should be concentrating on thinking skills, design skills, people skills, and so on.

Universities are excellently placed to do wonderful things for society. They just need to have the will to do them.

8   Schools

Schools in the European Union spend 25 per cent of their teaching time on mathematics. But most people only use about 3 per cent of the mathematics they learn at school. I have never consciously used the geometry, algebra, trigonometry, differential calculus or integral calculus I learned at school.

So why do we spend this rather high portion of school time on the more advanced 97 per cent of mathematics?

Because a student may want to enter a profession that does require this grounding in mathematics.
If you wanted to be a rocket scientist, you could learn the necessary mathematics as part of that course. This applies to many professional choices. There is no need for everyone else to learn so much mathematics.

Because it trains the mind.
I am not aware of any evidence that shows that those who

studied more mathematics, or were better at it, have superior minds compared with those who studied less. It may indeed have some effect, but if the intention was to train the mind, then there are many much more powerful things we could do to train the mind and to train thinking. There are aspects of my thinking that have been shown to have a powerful effect, increasing performance in every subject by between 30 and 100 per cent; improving employment chances by 500 per cent; reducing violence by 90 per cent. Can anyone claim such results for mathematics?

Because some mathematics is needed so more mathematics must be better.
The tradition has been established and is continued and defended.

Because it is necessary to fill the time allocated to 'baby-sitting' in education.
Youngsters need to be occupied. Mathematics, like many other subjects, simply fills their time.

I am certainly not against teaching mathematics, but if education claims not to have the time to teach other subjects, such as thinking, then the amount of time spent on mathematics could be reduced.

There is also another aspect. Students who are not good at mathematics may leave school feeling they are stupid. Their self-esteem is very low, and this affects both their future lives and their contribution to society.

THINKING

Teaching thinking should be the key subject in education. Nothing is more important than thinking – for personal life, for professional life and for contributions to society.

To claim that schools already teach thinking as part of teaching other subjects like history and science is a very weak argument. To be sure, some thinking is taught, but it is mainly of the analytical type.

There is a real need to teach broad operational thinking skills. There is a need to teach *perceptual thinking* – which is extremely important and will be considered later. There is a need to teach genuine *exploratory thinking* – not argument. There is a need to teach *value thinking*. There is a need to teach *action thinking*. There is a need to teach *creative thinking*.

John Edwards, a research teacher in Australia, reduced the amount of time at school devoted to science, and taught some thinking in that time. In the science examinations those students who had been taught some thinking did better than those students who had spent more time on science. He also showed that teaching thinking doubled the number of students getting to the top level in mathematics.

Another report, from India, showed that teaching thinking greatly improved performance in mathematics.

Thinking needs to be taught explicitly as a separate subject. Youngsters who may not be good at other subjects suddenly find they are good thinkers, and their self-esteem rises with powerful effect.

I have had many reports from teachers along the following lines: 'I thought Suzy was not very bright because she did not perform well. But in the thinking lessons she blossomed, to the surprise of myself and all the other students.' I have had reports from China about students who suddenly found that they were expected to think instead of just learning what they were supposed to learn. They found this a liberating experience.

I am concerned with constructive thinking, which is why in the days of the Soviet Union and in Communist Bulgaria there was a lot of interest in my work. In my experience Communist regimes were not at all against thinking and new ideas. This is also the case in China today where the government is trying out pilot projects with my work in five provinces.

On one occasion in the Soviet Union I was asked to teach in School 36 in Moscow. At first the students were very quiet, but gradually they realised they were allowed to have ideas, and the noise level rose and rose.

In Bulgaria I was told the story of a young girl from Plovdiv (the second largest town in Bulgaria). She was asked if she used the thinking lessons in her daily life. She answered: 'I use these things all the time in my daily life. I even use them outside life – in school.'

Just that one sentence summarises the need to teach thinking in schools.

Research on thinking in schools

Denise Inwood of the Atkey organisation has done extensive research on the teaching of these methods in schools in the United Kingdom. Susan Mackie of the de Bono Institute in Melbourne, Australia, has also done a lot of work with schools. Tom Farrell of the de Bono Foundation in Dublin is also involved.

The evidence is clear. Teaching thinking explicitly as a separate subject improves performance in every other subject by between 30 and 100 per cent.

Many years ago there was some research done by the Schools Council in the UK. It claimed to show that teaching this thinking did not increase the number of ideas produced.

For this research, one group of pupils was taught my PMI technique, and another group was simply told by the teacher to come up with as many ideas as possible. There was no difference between the groups' results. The conclusion was drawn from this.

In my opinion, that is poor research. First of all, the PMI is not a creative technique at all. It simply asks the student to consider the Plus, Minus and Interesting points about a matter. It is for perceptual clarification, not creative thinking. Because there are other techniques of mine that are designed to be creative, it was incorrectly assumed that the PMI was also creative.

It was also shown that the group just coming up with ideas had more irrelevant ideas than the PMI group. So although the overall number of ideas was similar, one lot included many irrelevant ideas.

I believe this research is highly dangerous because it may have discouraged many educators from trying my methods for themselves. Helen Hyde of the Watford Grammar School for Girls has, however, used the methods extensively with very positive results.

In Venezuela, every child in every school learns my methods. This was the result of the work of Luis Alberto Machado, who was originally a professor of philosophy at the University of Caracas. He read my book *The Mechanism of Mind* and later joined the Copei party, which was in government. He requested a new ministry – for the Development of Intelligence. He became Minister for the Development of Intelligence.

He then came to see me in London to ask what should be done. I told him I had a programme for schools to teach perceptual thinking. This was the CoRT (Cognitive Research Trust) programme. He invited me to Venezuela where I trained 250 teachers. They then in turn picked up some experience, and trained 107,000 more teachers. The programme finally passed into the Ministry of Education and became mandatory in all schools.

Every country needs a Minister for the Development of Intelligence if the human resources in that country are not to be wasted by inadequate education methods. It is not enough to rely on Ministers of Education to make the needed changes.

OTHER SUBJECTS

Many schools are already teaching the use of computers, the Internet and other aspects of information technology. There are, however, other subjects listed below which are equally important. How is space going to be made when the curriculum is already so crowded?

These subjects are so key that there needs to be a change in how much time is spent on traditional subjects compared to these subjects. As discussed, the amount of time spent on mathematics can be reduced. Subjects like history and geography can be taught with videos downloaded from the Internet. Language and thinking can be integrated together. Less time can be spent on literature.

Operacy

Literacy and numeracy are not enough. A mass of knowledge is not enough. As soon as a youngster gets out into the world, there is a need to 'do' and to 'get things done'. Operacy is all about the skill of doing or operating.

Youngsters can be given tasks and projects to plan and to carry out. A side effect of this is the sense of achievement when something gets done. This is very important, because youngsters do not have much opportunity for achievement. Operacy may include doing things on your own or as a team, such as in the Young Enterprise scheme. There needs to be a mixture of both.

Design

This is part of thinking but needs direct attention. Design tasks can be set. These can be carried out in reality or shown in a drawing. Youngsters can make a drawing showing how to build a house more quickly; how to improve a motor car; how to wash windows in a skyscraper; how to design a supermarket.

Design is putting things together to deliver value. This is very different from analysis and description. Design is not drawing pretty pictures of a cottage with hollyhocks outside. Designs can be compared and discussed. Practicality and other values can be commented upon.

Systems behaviour

There are schools in some parts of the world that do teach simple systems behaviour. This is a very useful way for youngsters to get a sense of how things interact. There can be a basic understanding of positive feedback and negative feedback, amplifying systems, and so on. There is no need to get into very complex matters. What is needed is a sense of how things interact and come together to produce a result. Studying items on their own is not enough.

The world around

This involves an understanding of how shops work; how unions work; how governments work; how the UN is supposed to work; how the media works. It involves some knowledge of how things function and interact. This need not be an in-depth knowledge. There may even be games that youngsters can play to give this understanding.

SUMMARY: SCHOOLS

There is a great deal that needs to be done to improve education, but it is rather unlikely to happen. This is because education advisers and consultants have been brought up in the old traditions and want to preserve them. Continuity is the name of the game.

Education is a classic example of a local equilibrium where all the elements are locked together to keep things as they are.

At the same time, there are so many new fads and fashions that education is being exhorted to adopt that a reluctance to change at all is understandable.

Even if an individual school wants to change, it still has the responsibility of getting its pupils through existing examinations, because that will affect their careers. Perhaps a new examination opportunity might be a good way to start change – what about an additional examination in thinking skills?

9 The Media

A report has shown that 56 per cent of young people in the United Kingdom do not trust the press. This may seem very alarming. It might be expected of older people with years of experiencing the games of the press, but it is rather alarming for young people to have this degree of mistrust.

Would this figure surprise or concern the media? I do not think so. I do not think the press ever expect to be trusted. What matters is a good story – even if only part of it is true, that is enough if the story sells.

At its best, the press is very, very good. At its worst, it is embarrassingly bad. There are some highly intelligent and honest journalists. There are many journalists who are either stupid or dishonest. It is difficult to tell which is which.

Early on in my career there was an excellent piece about my work by the *Sunday Times* Insight team. There was also a very good piece by Margaret Pringle. On the other hand, some time ago there was also a remarkably silly piece in a different newspaper. Did the journalist not realise that the facts she failed to mention were crucial and may also have interested the readers? Would the readers not have been interested to hear that teaching thinking in schools increased performance in every subject by between 30 and 100 per cent? Would the readers not be interested in learning that teaching thinking reduced crime among youngsters by 90 per cent?

The journalist did not, in my view, write a balanced article because important facts, namely the positive results, were not included, and the piece as a result reflects very poorly on the newspaper.

NEGATIVE

What that episode indicated to me is the stupidity of the press in general. Stupidity in believing that what interests the reader is negativity. To be sure, the press has a duty to expose scandals, corruption and bad behaviour, but the belief that readers are only interested in negative stuff is misplaced. There is a real need for much more positive stuff in the world.

The fundamental problem is that it is very much more difficult to write a positive piece than a negative piece. Much more talent is required, and some editors and journalists seem to lack such talent. So the end product is invariably negative. That hardly encourages positive attitudes or constructive thinking among readers.

In Australia they have what is called the 'tall poppy effect'. If you are walking through a field and there is a tall poppy that stands out above the rest, the temptation is to take your stick and lop the head off that poppy. The attitude is, of course, inherited from England and the days when society was rigidly structured into classes. Anyone who was seen to be getting above himself or trying to rise out of his or her class bracket had to be cut down to size. This silly attitude never developed in the USA, where success of any sort (even criminal) is respected.

WHAT CAN THE MEDIA DO?

Newspaper circulations are falling because of competition from television, the Internet and even social networks. If newspapers are to have any function in society, they need to develop positive products that television cannot easily offer because of the nature of the medium.

Reading is very powerful.

Research has shown that for women, eating chocolate, shopping and falling in love all have the effect of raising phenylethylamine in the blood and giving pleasure.

For men, eating curry, making money and looking at *Playboy* magazine all increase activity in the pleasure centre of the brain.

While it is interesting, this research is only partial, since there was a limit on what was tested. For both sexes, achievement, even minor achievement, is very satisfying. That is why crossword puzzles and Sudoku are so popular.

There are other ways of providing opportunities for achievement in newspapers.

SUMMARY: THE MEDIA

Celebrity culture is not in itself very stimulating mentally. Some celebrities have indeed shown talent in sport, music or acting. Others are famous for being famous in a positive feedback loop.

The media once played a central role in culture. That is hardly the case today.

10 Perception

This may well be the most important section in the whole of this book.

Perception is a key part of thinking. Professor David Perkins of Harvard University has shown in his research that 90 per cent of the errors in thinking are errors of perception. Logic plays only a small part. And no matter how excellent the logic might be, if the perception is faulty, the answer will be wrong. He told me: 'What you have been saying all along about the importance of perception is probably right.'

Goedel's Theorem proves that from within any system you can never logically prove the starting points – no matter how logical you might be. The starting points are arbitrary perceptions and assumptions that cannot be proved logically. So no matter how logical you think you are, your conclusion will be determined by your starting points, not the excellence of your logic.

LOGIC VS. PERCEPTION

If perception is indeed so very important in thinking, why have we totally neglected it? We are constantly emphasising logic, but logic without perception is misleading and can be very dangerous. Logic from a wrong perception can give the appearance of truth with a resulting action that can be dangerous.

The main reason is that the thinking determined by the Church in the early Middle Ages did not need perception. What was needed was truth, logic and argument to prove the heretics wrong. There was no need for perception because you were not dealing with the real world. You were dealing with artificial concepts designed by man and with a given definition that everyone could agree upon: the omnipotence of God; sin; fallibility, and so on. It was never a matter of perceiving the real world. Playing around with these 'designed' pieces needed logic. There was no place for perception and no need for perception.

PERCEPTION IN THE REAL WORLD

The real world of actual living is very different. We have not decided that there is no place for perception. Perception is more important than anything else. But we have done nothing about it.

Another reason why we have neglected perception is

that we did not know what to do about it. Applying logic to perception did not work – because it was a different system.

In Australia, a five-year-old boy called Johnny was offered a choice by his friends between a one-dollar coin and a two-dollar coin. The one-dollar coin was much bigger than the two-dollar coin. Johnny took the bigger coin. His friends laughed and giggled at Johnny's stupidity. Whenever they wanted to make a fool of Johnny, they would offer him the same choice. He never learned. He always chose the larger coin.

One day an adult saw this and felt sorry for Johnny. He called Johnny over and told him that the smaller coin, even though smaller, was actually worth twice as much as the bigger coin.

Johnny smiled and thanked him politely and then said: 'I know that. But how many more times would they have offered me the coins if I had chosen the two dollars the first time?'

It was a matter of perception. If you saw it as a single occasion, you would take the two dollars. If you knew your friends, as Johnny did, you would know that they would keep on offering the coins and you would get many dollar pieces. Perception is key.

Jilly Cooper, the well-known novelist, once wrote a piece in a newspaper suggesting that if you wanted to know if your man had another woman, you should note the length of his tie when he left after breakfast and the length of the tie when he returned in the evening. One day a fellow returns home with his tie at a much shorter length than when he left in the morning. His wife has a go at him, accusing him of seeing some other lady.

'Honey, I have been playing squash,' he replies. You have to take off your tie to play squash. The lady's perception changes and with it her emotions.

Logic will never change emotions, but changing perception will always change emotions. You have no option.

As mentioned earlier, in the Karee mine in South Africa, some of my simple techniques for changing perception were taught (by Susan Mackie and Donalda Dawson) to the illiterate miners. Among the simple perception tools is the OPV acronym, which asks the thinker to consider the Other Person's View. Carrying out this simple mental task reduced the conflicts between the seven tribes working there from 210 a month to just four.

We are constantly emphasising logic, but logic without perception is misleading and can be very dangerous. Logic from a wrong perception can give the appearance of truth with a resulting action that can be dangerous.

POSSIBILITIES AND ALTERNATIVES

A man seems to be coming towards you with an aggressive look on his face. What are the possibilities?

- He really is aggressive.
- That is the natural set of his face and he is not aggressive at all.
- For some reason he feels threatened and insecure and this is his reaction.
- He is showing off with a bit of bravado – perhaps to impress his friends.
- He is fooling around.
- He is not making his way towards you at all but towards the person standing right behind you.

Some of these alternative possibilities are not as likely as others, but perception demands the generation of possibilities. We then make an effort to check out all the possibilities.

Our minds naturally want to jump as quickly as possible to the conclusion of 'truth' and 'certainty', because that will determine our action. As a result, our perceptions are very often mistaken and our action will also be mistaken.

Objects and situations

We can recognise a dog, a car, a horse, a tree. The different features lead to the name or word. Situations are more complex. We do not have names for different situations, so they are more difficult to recognise. As mentioned elsewhere in this book, I have created a coding system to allow us to give names to complex situations. Even so, we may be mistaken.

You are unlikely to have to say: 'This could be a horse or a car.' It will be clear. But you may well have to say: 'It could be this situation or that situation.' In perception, we always have to keep alternatives and possibilities in mind. This is much less so for familiar objects, but it is essential for situations, where we might more easily be mistaken.

WHAT CAN WE DO?

What can we do about perception? What can improve our perceptual thinking?

This is an area about which we have done virtually nothing for 2,400 years because we have been so obsessed with the excellence of logic.

There are at least three things we can do:

1. Attitude
2. Perceptual tools
3. Perceptual maps

Attitude

Much of the attitude needed has already been described.

We need to acknowledge the huge importance of perception.

We need to realise that logic is not enough. We need to realise that logic can never be better than the perceptions on which it is based.

There are a number of attitudes, habits and mental operations that are needed for thinking. These are in addition to the specific tools and enhance the effectiveness of these tools.

There is the basic attitude that you can seek to be creative about anything. There is a need to get away from the problem-solving attitude that focuses on failures, faults and shortcomings. These do need thinking about and the lateral thinking tools may be used for that purpose. The great danger is that we limit our creative thinking to problems. This means that we make no attempt to generate new possibilities if something seems to be working well. This is reflected in the well-known phrase 'If it is not broken, don't fix it'.

Another fundamental attitude is the willingness to use 'movement' rather than 'judgement'. Our normal thinking, for obvious reasons (and important ones), is all about judgement. Judgement exists on many levels. Is this relevant? Is this useful? Is this correct? Will this work?

Instead of judgement we try to use 'movement'. This is a very different mental operation. Judgement is all about 'accept' and 'reject' in addition to 'recognition'. Movement is all about movement: where can I move to from this position? We seek to move forwards and to use things for their movement value.

The actual process of movement is described earlier, but what is important is to be able to look at anything for its 'movement value' and not just its usual judgement value. That requires a big change in attitude.

Another attitude is the willingness to look for alternatives. This means making an effort to go beyond the obvious alternatives to seek further ones. There may be alternatives of perception: how else could we look at this? There may be alternatives of explanation: what are the alternative explanations for what is happening? There may be alternatives for action: what alternative courses of action do we have? There may be alternatives for choice: what are the options? There can be alternatives in many areas. There can be alternative consequences of an action. There can be alternative scenarios.

Being open to alternatives means not being in a hurry to arrive at the 'truth' or the 'best'.

Linked to the search for alternatives is the attitude that opens up and accepts possibilities. Too often science has been frozen because of a claimed truth (such as the belief that peptic ulcers were caused by stomach acid). There is a skill in being practical and action orientated and, at the same time, keeping possibilities in mind. In a marriage you have to choose one lady or man from among many possibilities. You are then supposed to forget about the possibilities. With creativity you need to keep possibilities active even while you get on with practicalities.

We need to consider possibilities and alternatives and to keep these in mind – instead of jumping to a conclusion.

We need to realise that other people may have other perceptions based on their experience and values.

Perceptual tools

An explorer is sent off to a newly discovered island. On his return he makes a report. He comments on the smoking volcano in the north of the island. He comments on a strange-looking bird that cannot fly.

He is asked for further comments. He replies that these were the only things that caught or 'pulled' his attention.

This is not good enough. He is sent back to the island with specific instructions to 'direct' his attention rather than waiting for it to be 'pulled' in some direction. He is asked to look north and to note down all he sees. Then he should look east and note down what he sees. Then south and then west.

He returns with a much fuller description of the island. This is because he had a framework for 'directing attention' rather than relying on something to catch or 'pull' his attention.

In the same way someone is sent into the garden to look at all the colours. The dominant colours will 'pull' their attention – the yellow in daffodils, the green in grass. Less-obvious colours will be ignored. However, if that same person is sent into the garden with a framework to look for each colour in turn – blue, yellow, red, brown – their attention scan will be far more comprehensive.

Attention is a key element in improving perception. If

we don't direct attention, we see only the familiar patterns.

So what can we do about directing attention instead of waiting for our attention to be pulled towards something, usually something unusual? In my book *Six Frames for Thinking about Information* I noted that we could set directions in which to look and in each case note what we see in that direction. We can look for value, for interest, for accuracy, for satisfaction, etc.

In exactly the same way we can create formal frameworks for 'directing attention' which function like the NSEW (North-South-East-West) framework and which improve perception.

This forms the basis of the CoRT (Cognitive Research Trust) programme for thinking that is now widely used in tens of thousands of schools worldwide. There are 60 lessons in the full CoRT programme. Not all of these are perceptual tools. For instance, CoRT 4 is mainly about creativity. The most basic perceptual tools are in CoRT 1. In addition to these specific tools, the key factor in perception is possibilities and alternatives. You are looking at the situation in one way and you examine other possibilities and alternatives.

Basic tools

PMI: This means directing attention to the Plus (positive) aspects, then the Minus (negative) aspects and finally the

Interesting aspects. 'Interesting' means something worth noting or commenting upon. What is interesting here? That aspect may be neither positive nor negative.

CAF (pronounced 'caff'): Considering All Factors. The thinker makes a deliberate effort to see all the factors that are relevant to the thinking. What should be taken into account?

C&S: This means directing attention to the Consequences and Sequels, whichever there may be. What will happen in the future? What are the immediate consequences, the short-term consequences, the medium-term consequences and the long-term consequences? These may not be easy to see – but the effort must be made.

AGO: Aims, Goals and Objectives. We usually have only a vague idea of what we are trying to do. The AGO asks us to be very clear. What are we trying to achieve? What is the goal? What are the objectives? Spelling these things out is very different from just having them in the back of the mind.

FIP (pronounced 'fipp'): This tool directs attention to the First Important Priorities. Not everything is of equal importance. In any list some things are more impor-tant than others. This tool directs attention to the important things and the priorities. It also directs attention to what must be done, or considered, first.

APC: Alternatives, Possibilities and Choices. What are the alternatives here? They may be alternatives of explanation, alternatives of perception and alternatives of action. What are the possibilities? What are the choices, both the obvious choices and the more hidden ones? This tool seeks to multiply possibilities.

OPV: Other People's Views. Here the thinker seeks to get inside the mind of the other parties involved to see what their thinking might be. Very often this tool dissolves fights and conflicts. It is the main tool that reduced the fights in the Karee mine. There is a genuine effort to see where the other person is coming from. It is never a matter of what the other person *should* be thinking, but of what the other person *might* be thinking.

There are other tools in the full CoRT programme, including tools for identifying values, and tools for identifying the information available and the information that is missing.

Examples of the basic tools

The PMI tool: Asks the thinker to direct his or attention first to the Plus aspects of the matter. Then attention is directed to the Minus aspects and finally to the Interesting aspects.

A class of thirty 12-year-old boys in Australia were asked

to consider the suggestion that youngsters should be paid for going to school. In groups of four they discussed the idea. At the end, all 30 of them agreed that it would be a great idea: they could buy comics, sweets, chewing gum, movie tickets, and so on.

Then the PMI was explained to them. Again in groups of four they went systematically through the different attention directions: Plus, Minus and Interesting. At the end of this exercise, 29 out of the 30 had changed their minds and decided that it was not a good idea to pay youngsters for going to school.

The Plus points were as they had been before. But now there were Minus points. The bigger boys might bully the younger boys for the money. The school might raise the charge for lunch in response. Parents would be less inclined to give presents. They asked where the money would be coming from and suggested there might be a greater need elsewhere in education. There were also some Interesting points. They wondered whether the amount would be varied as a sort of punishment. Or if older students would get more.

The important point is that there was no teacher intervention at all. The teacher simply laid out the PMI framework that the youngsters used. As a result of using the framework they got a broader perception and changed their minds. This is precisely what the teaching of thinking should be about: providing tools that can be used to make a difference.

The C&S tool: I was once giving a seminar to a group of very senior female executives in Canada. I asked them to consider the suggestion that women should be paid 15 per cent more than men for doing the same job. They discussed the idea in small groups and decided that it made sense because women had more responsibilities (family, for example). Eighty-six per cent declared themselves in favour of the idea.

I then asked them to use another attention-directing tool called the C&S. This stands for Consequences and Sequels. It directs attention to the immediate consequences, the short-term consequences, the medium-term consequences and the long-term consequences. They went through the exercise. At the end, with whatever reasons they had come up with, the 86 per cent in favour of the idea had fallen to just 15 per cent in favour.

The important point about this example is that if you had asked any of those women executives if they looked at consequences, they would have replied that in their role as senior executives they spent most of their time looking at consequences. Yet doing it deliberately with the C&S tool made a huge difference.

The APC tool: Asks for attention to be directed to Alternatives, Possibilities and Choices. Down's syndrome youngsters are able to use these tools very effectively. It may be that in this condition there is a difficulty in one part of the brain giving instructions to another part. So they make a hand sign for the tool they want to use. These hand signs were developed in the mines in South Africa, where the noise makes talk difficult.

So the youngster might make the hand sign for APC and then he reacts to his own hand sign and carries out an APC. By exteriorising the instruction, the Down's syndrome youngster can overcome any difficulty with internal instruction.

These things are so simple and so obvious that everyone claims to do them all the time. Time and again, experiments like those mentioned above show that directing attention deliberately with these simple tools makes a huge difference.

Attitude is not the same as using a formal tool. Most people would claim to have a balanced attitude and to look for both the positive and the negative aspects of a situation. In fact we do this in a very perfunctory way. And we do not do it at all when we like or dislike the situation immediately. How often have you made an effort to find the Plus points of someone you dislike?

As I mentioned earlier, an educator once said that these tools were so simple they could not possibly work. But they do work, and very powerfully. You need to understand how the brain operates in order to see why they should work.

Many people have said that the tools simply give acronyms to aspects of normal behaviour. Others like the methods but object to the acronyms.

The acronyms are essential as acronyms are stored in the brain. Attitudes have no location in the brain. They are like an itinerary put together by a travel agent. You cannot switch on an attitude at will.

The acronyms have a place in the brain just as names of things have a place in the brain. A man had a stroke, and the only effect was that he could not remember the names of vegetables. The stroke had damaged that area of the brain where the names of vegetables were stored. In the same way, acronyms are stored and can be called into action, just like a computer programme.

Perceptual maps

The Flowscape

In my book *Water Logic* I describe the Flowscape, which is a way of mapping out or displaying perceptions.

If you are travelling down the river on a boat, town A is followed by town B. Town C might come next. Town A does not 'cause' town B. One simply follows the other.

A 'neural state' in the brain is stable for a while, and then the 'tiring factor' takes effect and the next stable state (of sensitised neurones) takes over. So there is a movement from one state to another. It is not necessarily to do with causation or inclusion; as with the river, one thing follows another.

With a Flowscape you simply list a number of elements that you see in the total situation (not necessarily at any one moment in time).

Then, for each point on that list, you see to which other point on the list your mind would most readily move. Every point must have one, and only one, arrow leading to another point. A point may receive many arrows but can only emit one arrow.

Then you map it out. You may find that points you thought were central are actually peripheral. You may find points that reinforce each other. You get a visual display that allows you to look at the elements in your perception.

Flowscape points:

THINKING → EDUCATION
CHURCH → LOGIC
EDUCATION → LOGIC
ARGUMENT → LOGIC
LOGIC → GOEDEL
GOEDEL → PERCEPTION
PERCEPTION → POSSIBILITY
POSSIBILITY → CREATIVITY
CREATIVITY → POSSIBILITY
DESIGN → CREATIVITY

The mapped-out Flowscape is shown overleaf. It is easy to see two groupings. In one of them, Logic is central. In the other, Possibility is central. The movement from one grouping to another is via Goedel's Theorem (that logic can never be enough).

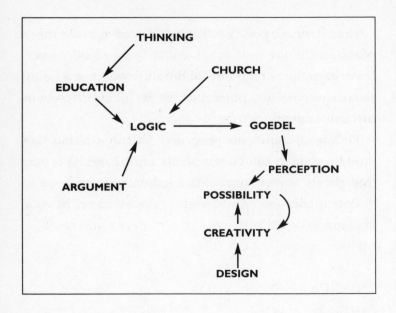

SUMMARY: PERCEPTION

Logic is not enough. Perception is very important. Indeed, in daily life perception is more important than logic. Yet we have done nothing about perception.

In this chapter I have sought to show that we *can* do something about perception. It is astonishing that we have had to wait 2,400 years for this.

For a final example, in an experiment, students were shown still photographs of two candidates who had run against each other in some election. No names or party affiliations were given. The students were asked to guess which of the two had won the election. The students were correct 70 per cent of the time. What are the implications of this?

Perhaps the perceptions of the students were so good that they could see confidence, ability and responsibility just from the still picture of a face.

Perhaps the students persuaded themselves that they could see these things but in the end chose what they thought the voters would have chosen.

Perhaps democracy has reached a point where physical appearance matters more than experience and ability.

11 Critical Thinking and Criticism

This section overlaps in part with other sections, such as argument and democracy. The subject is, however, important enough to deserve a chapter of its own.

Many of those teaching thinking today are focused on teaching 'critical thinking'. There are two aspects to consider here.

Some of those teaching critical thinking claim that it covers all types of thinking, including creativity. They claim that the word 'critical' simply means 'important', in the sense of a critical issue or a critical area. This is a dangerous and misleading use of the word. The word 'critical' comes from the Greek *kritikos*, which means 'judge'. So critical thinking is judgement thinking, and that is the usual meaning of the word. Private meanings have no validity.

The other aspect is that critical thinking takes us right back to where we started and what this book is about. The judgement thinking of the Greek Gang of Three (GG3) is excellent – but not enough. For the Church at the Renaissance critical thinking was enough because you simply judged whether something fitted standard doctrines or not.

In the real world, critical thinking is simply not enough. You may be so brilliant at critical thinking that you can destroy any silly idea, and even good ones. But no amount of critical thinking can produce new ideas in the first place. Where are new ideas to come from?

The repeated emphasis on critical thinking simply shuts the door on possibilities, new ideas and progress. There may be many people who will use their excellent critical thinking on the contents of this book – but can they design something better? The need is there.

We need perceptual thinking. We need design thinking. We need creative thinking. No amount of excellence at critical thinking will supply this need.

A motor car has brakes. These are essential. Without brakes you would be crashing all the time. But brakes are not enough. A motor car obviously needs an engine as well as brakes. The only time brakes might be enough would be if you were rolling down a hill on a very wide road. So critical thinking may be enough if we are in a state of decline – but not if we want to make progress.

CRITICISM AND COMPLAINT

Criticism and complaint are a necessary part of society. They are essential to prevent aberrations and to keep control.

Most people find complaint rather easy; they can even develop an indulgent habit of complaint.

Consumer groups brought together to help design new products and services are very good at pointing out the things that could be corrected or removed. At the same time the groups are not much good at suggesting new ideas, new products and new services.

While acknowledging the great importance of criticism and complaint, we need to make it very clear that this thinking is inferior to design thinking, creative thinking or discovery thinking. This needs to be made clear at school and at universities. The development of the 'critical mind' is simply not enough. It is even worse than that. Many excellent minds that might have been creative and able to contribute to society in that way are trapped and channelled into being excellent critical minds. This is largely the case with the media, where the critical mode often seems to be the only one used.

Nothing I have written here is intended to diminish the importance of critical thinking. It is excellent, but it is not enough. We need to be able to produce new ideas. Just waiting for chance to produce new ideas is much too slow.

If creative and design thinking had been part of our

education over the last few centuries, the world might be in a much more advanced state than it is.

PROBLEM-SOLVING

The term 'problem-solving' has done as much damage to the teaching of thinking as the term 'critical thinking' – and for the same reason. Both are excellent and essential – but they are not enough. They block development in other directions.

You are driving a car and it breaks down. That provides you with two problems. The first is how to get to where you need to go, and the second is how to fix the broken-down car.

The boat has a leak. That is a problem and you have to fix it.

This new drug for arthritis seems to increase the risk of heart attack. That is a problem that has to be fixed.

There is a problem child who will not do as he is told. How do you fix that problem?

A problem is a deviation from the normal or a deviation from the expected. Thinking to solve problems is very important – but it is not enough.

You have a task to carry out. How do you do it? That is not itself a problem, although there may be problems along the way.

You want to improve something? That is not a problem.

Those who claim that the term 'problem-solving' covers everything suggest that 'anything you want to do' forms a problem. So any intended mental activity is a problem.

This is misleading and dangerous. It is misleading because it suggests that the only sort of thinking is problem-solving. It is dangerous because it excludes all the other sorts of thinking: design, creative, perceptual, and so on.

Business schools in the USA (and elsewhere) focus exclusively on problem-solving. This excludes the design of strategies and the creativity needed for things such as new alliances and new marketing concepts.

It is no use claiming, as is done for critical thinking, that the term problem-solving covers all sorts of thinking. It does not and it should not.

One of the major uses of creativity is simplicity. Over time procedures and operations get ever more complex. While there is a natural tendency to ever more complexity, there is no natural tendency towards simplicity.

I suggested in my book *Simplicity* some years ago that the British government should abolish passport control on leaving the UK. At the time, if someone was found to have overstayed their visa, they were arrested, taken to court, then deported. Why not just allow them to leave and wave goodbye in the first instance? Three months after the publication of the book, passport control on leaving the UK was abolished.

When I came up with this idea, I was not seeking to solve a problem. The system worked as it stood.

Improvement and simplification is not problem-solving. Simplicity saves time, money, hassle and stress. Using creativity to simplify something deliberately is one of the most important practical uses of creativity.

The real danger of treating thinking as problem-solving is that we only focus our attention on problems and deficiencies. What is not a 'problem' does not get our thinking attention.

DEFECTS

I was invited to talk at a large education meeting in Italy. There were about 10,000 teachers present. Almost the whole meeting was about teaching difficult or disadvantaged students (with conditions such as autism). It was assumed that everything else in education was perfect and did not need thinking about. I told them that our thinking was far from perfect and needed a great deal of attention.

It is the same with foundations. If I went to a large foundation, such as the Melinda and Bill Gates Foundation, or the Rockefeller Foundation, to ask for funds for dealing with AIDS in Africa, I might possibly get a grant. If I went and asked for funds to continue my work to improve the apparent best of human thinking, I doubt if I would be successful.

The habit of looking only at problems means that we

stagnate. As discussed earlier democracy could do with a lot of improvement, but you could not call it a 'problem'.

SUMMARY: CRITICAL THINKING AND CRITICISM

This very dangerous habit of calling all human thinking 'problem-solving' severely limits our attention to thinking and our use of thinking. Psychologists are among the worst offenders here – perhaps because they do not operate in the real world where a great deal of other thinking is needed. Problem-solving, like critical thinking, is excellent – but it is not enough.

Excellent but not enough is the theme in many sections of this book. It is not only that there are other things that need doing. The danger is that all other activity is blocked by our reverence for these things. At the same time I am not going to attack them and say that these things are wrong. They are not – they are excellent. But they drain attention and energy from other areas that need energy and attention.

12   Art and Thinking

The best-known statue of a thinker is that by Rodin. This statue is heavy, gloomy and boring. I would like to run an international competition for a statue of a thinker that showed excitement, achievement and hope. Thinking is not boring, tedious and heavy.

Art has done very little to encourage thinking. This is because art seems to believe that the true essence of human beings is emotion. Literature and theatre is usually about emotion, because that is where the drama lies. There is very little thinking and very little happiness.

I once suggested in Hollywood (through a page in *Variety* magazine) that a 'Happiness' rating be given to films. A very happy film would get HHHH, a less happy one HHH, then HH and finally one H. So when you were deciding which movie to go to, this rating could help your choice. I quickly got the impression that the movie industry did not like this idea at all. That may be because most films are anguished or full of fighting. It is probably because they realised that 'happy' films are not easy to make. Just as the press cannot escape from the easy option of negativity, so the movie-makers find it difficult to escape from the easy option of anguish and violence.

NEGATIVE IS REAL

There is a false belief that anguish and tragedy are the real essence of life. All else is superficial and distraction. This may indeed be true in terms of audience interest, but at the same time it is a powerful con trick that is not related to daily life. The tragedy element in most people's lives is tiny compared to the boredom element.

Being depressed sinks you into more depression. You need to think your way out of depression and also out of boredom.

DIFFERENT

Too many creative people believe that creativity is being different for the sake of being different. This applies very strongly to the area of painting. You do not want to paint as people did in the past, possibly because you would not do it as well. So you paint in a very different, even bizarre, fashion. You then persuade people of the value of your work – if they learn to look at it in the right way.

This is a perfectly valid operation; it has produced Cubism and Picasso as well as many excellent artists of today.

In addition, many artists are not creative per se; they are powerful stylists who have a valuable style of perception and expression. Many artists even become trapped in a certain style because it is what the world has come to expect of them. For example, an Andy Warhol piece of art was expected to look like an Andy Warhol piece of art.

Painting is really a choreography of attention. Attention goes to this point, then the whole, then back to another point. It is this dance of attention that is aesthetically pleasing. It is not unlike a music of attention. This is usually done unconsciously – but could also be done consciously.

Some painting and sculpture demands that the viewer do a lot of work before he or she can see a value. There is nothing wrong with that provided there is success at the end.

There are paintings that stimulate the viewer to think and that provide insights and understandings that were not there before. Such paintings are aids to perception and amplify our repertoire of perception possibilities.

CREATIVITY AND ART

Artists can be fresh and original, but they do not always have the flexibility that is part of creative thinking. It is true that they often have a willingness to play around with concepts and perceptions and a readiness to let the end result justify the process of getting there instead of following a series of set steps. All of this is important in the general creative mood.

However, there is a misperception that creativity has to do with art and therefore artists are the best people to teach creativity. That is like saying that the Grand Prix racing driver is the best designer of Grand Prix cars and the best driving instructor. There is a thought that there will be a sort of osmosis effect – the attitudes of the artist will come through to the students who will in turn become creative.

There are some artists who are creative and are good teachers of creativity. But these are people who are creative and are good teachers of creativity. They just happen to be artists. The confusion of 'creativity' with 'art' is a language problem and it can do much damage.

MUSIC

On the whole, music is much more uplifting than other forms of art. This covers classical music, and rock music, pop and modern too.

As a matter of interest, musicians have shown more interest in my work than other artists. This may be because in writing and painting you are representing something – even if remotely. In music you are creating the entire work, you are not just depicting something.

So operations such as 'provocation' make a lot of sense to musicians.

SUMMARY: ART AND THINKING

It could be claimed that life is to be experienced and not thought about. It could be claimed that the purpose of art is to make more acute that experience of life. I would not disagree with this.

At the same time, adding thinking to experience is like adding colour to a black-and-white photograph. Nuances, meaning and relationships now become visible.

Raw experiences and raw emotions are rather like raw meat, which is fine for those who like it.

13 Leadership and Thinking

It is almost impossible for a leader to talk about the importance of thinking. It has to be assumed that his or her thinking is near perfect. Furthermore, to talk about thinking makes the leader very vulnerable, as any policy or action can be attacked on the grounds that it shows poor thinking. So leaders do not talk about thinking.

The Prophet Muhammad probably had more to say about thinking than any other religious leader. In the Hadith, his own words as distinct from the Koran, the Prophet Muhammad has the following things to say:

'One hour of thinking is worth more than seventy years of prayer.' [This is thinking about the works of the Creator.]

'The ink of a scholar is more holy than the blood of a martyr.'

'One learned man gives more trouble to the Devil than one thousand worshippers.'

I was told by a person from the Ministry of Education in Saudi Arabia that there are 130 verses in the Koran about thinking.

When Jesus was in Jerusalem, he could not really talk about 'thinking', because this would have suggested the Pharisees (the academic, educated, lawyer class) – who were the bad guys – to his listeners. Muhammad in the desert could tell his warriors – who had no academic pretensions – that thinking was important.

COMPLACENCY

If you speak French and you live in France, why should you consider that any other language is important?

If you have set up the game of logic and play it very well, why should you consider that any other type of thinking is important?

If, as an educator, a university head or a Minister of Education, you believe that the traditions of the past are perfect, why should you consider that we have not really done very much about thinking since the GG3?

If you yourself have done very well with the existing modes of thinking, why should you encourage others to learn further modes?

If you live in innocent ignorance of the other modes of thinking, how can you be anything but complacent about thinking?

Far from encouraging further developments in human thinking, the leadership in education is more often minded to block such developments. Even if practical evidence shows the powerful effect of teaching perceptual thinking and creative thinking, the comfort of complacency, helped by traditional advisers, is more appealing.

It is usually individual teachers or individual school principals (like Helen Hyde of the Watford Grammar School for Girls) who have taken the initiative in making things happen.

Is this likely to change? Probably not.

NEW DIRECTIONS

When I was working on my book *The Mechanism of Mind*, I invented a new type of mathematics to deal with patterns, paths, and so on. I called it 'hodics', from the Greek *odos*, 'road'. Sometimes it is necessary to design new ways of tackling a subject.

Instead of our existing judgement-based thinking system of 'boxes' and categories, we may move towards a very different system. This would be a 'field effect' system, which would be much closer to the way the brain actually works. I shall be working on this. At the same time computers might come to be programmed to operate in a 'field effect' manner rather than digitally.

We may come to develop a new language for thinking. We certainly need a new language for perception. This would be softer and less hard-edged than our existing language. It would be like the contours of a landscape rather than the solidity of a building.

Instead of having to see someone as a 'friend' or an 'enemy', we might see the person as a complex of different factors. It may be appropriate to treat that person as an 'enemy' for the moment, but that does not mean that the person 'is' an enemy.

In the end we have to make decisions and take practical action – but judgements do not have to be permanent and irreversible. In politics there may be two people who hate each other's guts, but they know that they need each other and so have to work together.

THE CODES

The codes that I have developed will allow us to perceive the world in new ways. We will be able to communicate complex situations instantly. The codes will affect our habits of thinking. They may even allow thinking functions that we cannot carry out with ordinary language.

There is much to do in the design of better human

thinking. The first steps have been taken, but there is still a long way to go.

SEPTINES

This is a new aid to thinking that is being introduced in this book. This is the first time that I am writing about it. It is a way of considering a subject. Like many of the other methods of thinking, it is based directly on the way the brain works.

In the brain, a cluster of interconnected neurones will be active at a given moment. This cluster will eventually tire and the activity will move on to the next cluster that is ready to become active. This other cluster will have been sensitised, or made ready, by connections to the first cluster or by events in the outer world.

With the Septine we seek to make use of this behaviour. We activate different areas one after the other without in any way seeking to make connections. This means that there will be a number of sensitised areas in the brain. The effect of these may be to sensitise further areas. In this way new ideas or a clarification of ideas on a subject will come about.

In a Septine you simply note down seven different thoughts about the situation. There is no attempt at a logical sequence. These are scattered thoughts. They may be expressed as a single word, as a phrase or even as a sentence. Each element in a Septine exists in its own right.

There is no attempt to carry out an analysis or survey of the situation. It is just seven 'points' that are seen.

Holidays

A Septine on the design of holidays:

- change
- low hassle
- relax
- interest
- different
- comfort
- travel

You read through these seven points quite slowly. You can read them over and over again.

Many ideas might arise. There is no perfect Septine – they are subjective. Here is one of them:

A holiday with no travel at all. You stay in the comfort of your own home. You can relax. An agency provides a cook and other staff to look after you. Most important of all, the agency provides an 'interesting' house guest. This house guest could be an instructor or someone who could tell you about some particular area or experience.

That is the holiday design. You pay the agency.

Thinking

We can try a Septine on the subject of 'thinking'.

- action
- perception
- design
- thinking skill
- education
- experience
- opportunity

As before, there may be many possible ideas. Here is one of them:

Education should provide opportunities for direct experience. This experience will demand the use of thinking skill with regard to both perception of the situation and also the design for action.

In addition, the design of such experiences requires good design skills.

Not analysis

It is important to note that a Septine is not an analysis. The situation is not analysed into its parts. There are just different points, factors, considerations, observations that may be made. Different people may put together different Septines. The same person may put together a different Septine on another occasion – or even the same occasion.

Scatter

The 'scatter' element is very important in Septines. The points should not be closely connected but randomly put down. Not all the points have to be included in the final idea. The function of the points is just to sensitise different parts of the brain.

RECOGNITION

There is a reason for writing this section, and I will explain the reason at the end of the section.

A group of academics in South Africa put together a list of the 250 people who had contributed most to humanity since the beginning of time. I am on this list.

Many years ago I was awarded the Capire prize in Spain. More recently, the International Association of Management Consulting Firms gave me their top award, The Carl Sloane Award.

Some years ago the European Creative Association polled their members to ask who had most influenced them. It seemed that I came top of the list. They then asked the International Astronomical Union to suggest some award. The Union decided to name a minor planet after me. I believe this planet was discovered in 1973.

The government of Malta several years ago gave me the Order of Merit.

I have been on the Accenture (a leading business

consulting firm) list of the 50 most influential business thinkers in the world for many years. I believe I am currently at number 20 – even though my area is thinking, not business.

I am sometimes asked why there has been little recognition of my work in the UK, where I am based much of the time. I do not know the answer. I have dual British and Maltese citizenship. There are thousands of schools and millions of students around the world using my material. I would claim to have done more about idea creativity than anyone else in human history. I have published 82 books, translated into 41 languages (including Urdu, Korean, Romanian, etc.), and so on.

It has to be said that the UK honours system has been much discredited lately by reports of people buying honours by making a donation to party funds. The system is also used to reward popular heroes in order to secure votes. This means honours for rugby players, football players, rock musicians and actors. While these may be wonderful performers, they have hardly made a lasting contribution to humanity. Then there is the use of honours to reward public servants as a matter of routine.

I believe that it was a long time before the founder of the Internet (Tim Berners Lee) received any honour for one of the greatest inventions of the last century.

I once suggested a new award, to be called XARC. This would be for an Exceptional And Real Contribution. The first award would go to Mr Berners Lee for the Internet.

I did not have the time or energy to follow up on this initiative but the idea stands.

When I wrote my first book (called *The Use of Lateral Thinking* in the UK and *New Think* in the USA), the section of society that showed the most interest in thinking was the business community. This was the case even though that book had nothing directly to do with business.

This has been my experience ever since. Business has continued to be more interested in thinking, in general, than any other sector of society. The explanation for this is because there is a reality test. There is a bottom line. There are sales figures and profit figures. There are results. It is quite easy to tell how you are doing. If you are doing well you want to do better. If you are doing badly you need to do better. Business really needs to use creative thinking to succeed. Better and more creative thinking will result in more profits or market share.

I have many reports where some lateral thinking saved the corporations millions of dollars. David Tanner, who used to run the Center for Creativity at DuPont, tells a story of how a very short lateral thinking session saved $5 million. In another case the savings over a year were $87 million.

In Argentina, a man who ran a textile company started to teach my work to his employees. At that time he was half the size of his nearest competitor. Today, some years later, he is 10 times the size of that competitor.

In business there is an obvious need for new thinking. In most other sectors of society there is no bottom line. In all other sectors of society, such as politics, the media and the academic world, it is enough to argue and seek to prove verbally that you are right. There is no need at all for better thinking or creativity. In business you can argue until you are blue in the face that you are right – and still go bankrupt a month later.

I never set out to be an expert in business. I never pretend to be an expert in business. I am concerned with human thinking and with designing additional software for human thinking.

I do have to say, however, that in my experience the business sector is more interested in thinking than any other sector of society. You may not like that – but it is so. That is the reason for writing this section.

14 Conflicts and Disagreements

This is an area where the difference between traditional thinking and newer thinking becomes clear.

In a book I wrote on conflict resolution, I introduced the terms 'confliction' and 'de-confliction'. Confliction refers to the factors involved in the gradual build-up of a conflict before it becomes apparent as such. De-confliction is the removal of these factors.

There are two main types of conflict. These are 'bullying' and 'sillying'.

Bullying is when one party is oppressing another party for some gain to which it is not entitled. This is the sort of conflict that might elicit sanctions from the UN. The consequences of continued bullying need to be made uncomfortable. The design of better sanctions is a need here.

Sillying is when a conflict arises for no real reason. It may be a matter of national pride or something equally trivial. Conflict arises because the leaders on both sides have grown in importance by leading the conflict against the other side. These are usually leadership-grown conflicts even if there is sentiment supporting the leaders.

Our normal approach to conflicts is judgement, condemnation and attacking action.

The newer approach is to seek to design a way forward taking into account the needs, fears and future forecasting of both parties.

PERCEPTION

Even a thinking tool as simple as the OPV from the CoRT programme has a powerful effect in dissolving conflicts. Each party makes an effort to see the Other Person's View.

Among youngsters, fights simply dissolve when an OPV is carried out formally.

Having a clear view of the thinking of the other party makes all the difference. Emotions follow perception and action follows emotions.

EXPLORATION

Argument is a very poor way of settling a disagreement. 'A' has a point of view and 'B' disagrees. Argument simply hardens the existing positions and increases the sense of righteousness. They become more interested in winning or losing the argument than in the subject. Instead of argument, there is a need to explore the subject.

A corporation in Canada was about to have a strike. The Six Hats method of exploration was introduced. The strike was averted. A strike was also averted on a second occasion. In the end, the union said that they would not negotiate with management unless the Six Hats method was used.

The honest and objective examination of the situation by both sides is what is needed. In the Six Hats method, any dishonest or incomplete thinking becomes apparent to everyone. Cleverness in argument is no longer enough to support a position. Both 'A' and 'B' can wear the Black Hat at the same time to find out the dangers. Both 'A' and 'B' can wear the Yellow Hat to explore the benefits. Both 'A' and 'B' can wear the Green Hat to open up possibilities, etc.

Under the Black Hat, the grievances are put forward, the consequences of suggested action are examined. Under the Yellow Hat, the benefits of any possibility are made clear. The Green Hat is for alternatives, possibilities and modifications of an idea.

It is all very different from adversarial argument, which is about conflict transferred to the verbal level.

DESIGN

One of the underlying themes in this book is the difference between judgement and design.

Judgement is a look at what is – with a reference to the past.

Design is an arrangement of what could be – with a reference to the future.

Judgement claims to be about 'truth'. Design tries to be about 'value'.

For reasons ascribed to the Church in the Middle Ages, thinking has been exclusively about truth – to be arrived at by judgement. The idea of designing forward to create value has never been a formal part of the thinking culture.

Judgement examines and condemns individuals. Judgement examines and condemns actions. Once these judgement categories are decided, appropriate action follows. After all, if someone breaks the law, there is judgement followed by punishment.

Conflict situations, however, are very different from law-breaking – except in the person ready to judge.

We seek to design a way forward, taking into account the needs, greeds and fears of both parties.

TOOLS OF LATERAL THINKING

There may be a need for new concepts and new ideas. Here the formal tools of lateral thinking can be used.

We can use the tool of 'challenge' to challenge certain ideas and concepts that seem to be central to the conflict. We can seek alternatives.

The tool of 'concept extraction' can be used to find different ways to deliver a concept about which there is agreement.

The tool of provocation can be used to generate very different ideas.

The random entry tool is particularly useful when matters seem to have got stuck in a rut and no amount of ordinary thinking can shift them. The random entry tool can sometimes offer a completely different approach.

The more people are skilled in using these tools, the more successful will be the application of the tools.

SUMMARY: CONFLICTS AND DISAGREEMENTS

A conflict is not so much a problem as a situation that can develop one way or another.

Design and better thinking can help the situation develop in a positive way. Judgement simply freezes the situation.

15 Twenty-three Reasons Why Thinking Is So Poor

We can now summarise the reasons why world thinking is so poor. There is a certain amount of overlap between the reasons, but each reason needs to be considered in its own right if we are to make progress. Some of the reasons can also be grouped together.

SUCCESS IN SCIENCE AND TECHNOLOGY

Our huge success in science and technology makes us very proud of our thinking, complacent. Surely a thinking system that can produce such spectacular successes cannot be deficient? Unfortunately, the inanimate world of objects and effects is quite different from the animate world of people. In the inanimate world, properties are known, predictable and constant. This is not so when dealing with people.

People are unpredictable. There are also interactive loops, so behaviour of a certain type can itself change people's reactions. The nearest equivalent in science is the quark in physics, which changes its behaviour when observed.

Speaking French fluently in France does not mean that you would have an easy time in England.

We need to understand that different universes require different thinking.

NO FACULTY OR CLASSIFICATION

Most universities do not have a faculty of thinking. There is no Thinking classification in bookshops or most libraries. Thinking is the most fundamental of all human behaviour, but it does not get direct attention.

We walk and we talk and we breathe. It is assumed that thinking is as natural as these activities and does not merit any direct attention.

If no one is paying direct attention to thinking, how can things improve?

There is an astonishing degree of complacency in our habits and methods of thinking. This needs to change.

LEFT TO PHILOSOPHERS AND PSYCHOLOGISTS

Philosophers

It has always been assumed that it was the business of

philosophers and psychologists to look after human thinking. So no one else was concerned with thinking. Thinking was left to philosophers and logicians.

Philosophers had no option but to play word games. They would divide the world into perceptions and concepts and then explain how these interacted and fitted together. But these words and invented concepts adhered to the rules of logic – otherwise they would be seen as fantasy. The focus is on description and explanation. There is very little operational design. Operational tools mean thinking for action not description. And the huge importance of perception was not just neglected but ignored. Logic was enough.

From time to time philosophers do say useful things, but they do not set about designing better methods of thinking because they are too happy with the ones they have. And, because it was assumed, both in universities and elsewhere, that is was the territory of philosophers to deal with human thinking, no one else bothered. As a result virtually no progress was made for 2,400 years.

For example, we still believe that argument is a good way to explore a subject. Yet it is lengthy, crude, primitive and ineffective. There are much better ways, as described elsewhere in this book.

Psychologists

Psychology was in a hurry to prove that it was a real science like all the others. This meant measurement.

Measurement is objective. Measurement is the basis of all sciences; measurement is the difference between science and myth.

So psychology became obsessed with measurement, with various tests and scales. That obsession remains – from IQ tests to Myers-Briggs personality judgements. The outcome of these measurements is to put people into categories and boxes – introvert or extrovert; intuitive or judgemental – and thereafter they imprison themselves in the indicated box.

Once again, this has been descriptive, with very little design of operational thinking tools.

So, though all this thinking is excellent, it has very little to do with operational thinking.

IGNORANCE OF HOW THE BRAIN WORKS

A lack of understanding of how the brain works means that philosophers have been restricted to word games and psychologists to measurement.

Today we have an understanding of how the brain might work as a self-organising information system that creates asymmetric patterns. This is set out in my book *The Mechanism of Mind.* The concepts cannot be proved directly, but they provide the basis for designing thinking tools. These tools then have to prove their effectiveness when used. For example, one tool of lateral thinking –

the random word tool – generated 21,000 new ideas in an afternoon.

For the first time in human history, we have a logical explanation for idea creativity. We can then develop tools that can be used for deliberate creativity instead of having to wait for chance or sheer talent.

THE GREEK GANG OF THREE

The Greek Gang of Three (GG3) designed and set the software for our thinking today. They were, of course, Socrates, Plato and Aristotle. They did too excellent a job and we have been trapped by this excellence ever since.

Socrates was concerned with argument and questions. Plato was concerned with the truth. Aristotle created boxes, categories and recognition identification from which came our 'box logic'.

This was such an excellent system, at least compared with anything else around (in Europe), that it was eagerly taken up by scholars and thinkers. It remains our basic thinking software to this day. This type of thinking is indeed related to how the brain forms patterns. You identify the patterns and then apply standard behaviour for that pattern.

We need new thinking software for our brains.

PERCEPTION IGNORED

This is one of the most important points. We have ignored perception because we believed that logic was all. We now know that no amount of excellent logic can determine our starting perceptions (Goedel). If these perceptions are inadequate, then our outcome will be faulty – no matter how excellent the logic. We also know, from the research of David Perkins, that in ordinary life, 90 per cent of errors are errors of perception and not errors of logic at all.

Yet we persist in putting all the emphasis on logic and do nothing about perception. We can do a great deal about perception, as explained in this book, even with programmes as simple as the CoRT programme, which is now widely used in schools throughout the world.

RELIGION

It is not that religion has been anti-thinking. The problem is that religion has emphasised one type of thinking. This has effectively locked intellectual culture into the logic, truth and argument mode.

In religion there is no place for perception. That is given by doctrine, which has to be accepted through an act of faith. Once you have accepted this doctrine, then you can perceive the world through this framework.

In earlier days, disruptive thinkers were branded as heretics and even burned as such. Even Galileo, whose thinking was prompted by scientific observation and theory, fell foul of the Church.

Orthodoxy was what mattered – and this limits thinking. It is not so much the limitation on the contents of thinking that matters, but limitation on the actual methods of thinking, which had to remain stuck in the GG3 mode. We need to use new methods of thinking.

The Church

When Greek thinking (GG3) came into Europe at the Renaissance, schools, universities and thinking in general were in the hands of the Church. There was no need for creative thinking or design thinking. There was no need for perceptual thinking because the starting points were items of Church doctrine.

What the Church needed was truth, logic and argument with which to prove heretics wrong. Above all, though, the Church needed 'truth'. Without truth you could not believe. Without truth you could not persuade people to lead a better life. Without truth you could not burn heretics at the stake. The whole of thinking was directed to defending the truth. The starting places were given, defined and accepted. These were now juggled around with logic to prove the other party wrong.

So while logic, truth and argument became a central part of Western thinking culture, other aspects of thinking, such as design thinking, creative thinking, perceptual thinking and exploratory thinking, were completely ignored. It is interesting to note that Eastern religions often put more emphasis on perception and the way you could look at things. With Church thinking in the West, however, perceptual thinking, design thinking and creative thinking were not needed and so never became part of Western education. Our education system needs to change.

TRUTH AND POSSIBILITY

It has been noted that at one time science and technology in China were far ahead of what they were in the rest of the world. In a display of intellectual arrogance, Chinese scholars decided that truth and facts were enough. There was no place for the vagueness of the 'possibility system'. So progress came to a halt.

Even today, universities and other teaching institutions are very uncomfortable with possibility because it lies outside the limits of logic. They acknowledge the importance of the 'hypothesis' in science but only in a grudging way. There is no attempt to explore and make use of the power of possibility.

Possibility is essential for perceptual thinking. You have to consider alternative perceptions.

Possibility is essential for creative thinking.

Possibility is essential for design thinking.

Possibility is essential for exploratory thinking.

Because possibility was totally contrary to the needs of the Church at the Renaissance (a need for truth), it has been largely neglected in education.

Possibilities, hypotheses and alternatives need to be considered for our thinking to improve.

CRITICAL JUDGEMENT NOT DESIGN

'Critical' comes from the Greek word *kritikos,* which means 'judge'. The emphasis on teaching thinking, in the few places this happens, tends to be on critical thinking. This is excellent – but not enough. Our habits of thinking are all towards judgement. Recognise a standard situation and then you know what to do about it. Just like a doctor diagnosing a standard disease and prescribing the standard treatment.

We put a lot of emphasis on 'analysis', which is the method of breaking down complex situations so that we can identify standard elements – and so know what to do.

In a conflict situation we apply judgement at once. Who is the bad guy? What law or treaty has been violated? How can we put pressure on the bad guy? There is very little attempt to design a way forward.

Design is just as important as analysis but is almost totally neglected in education. Design is putting together what we have in order to deliver the values that we want. It is putting together fears, hopes, etc., to design a way forward. Design should be an integral part of education at all levels.

LANGUAGE

Language does not help. Language reinforces our judgement system and fixes our perceptions. We apply a word or label as soon as we can, and then this determines our perception (friend, enemy, and so on).

Language uses fixed boxes, and the identity device of 'is' excludes possibility and alternatives. We may need a softer language of perception where premature judgements can limit our thinking.

ARGUMENT

This is another very important point. We use argument far too much – because we have never developed another method of exploring a subject.

Argument is part of our critical and judgement mode of thinking. It was heavily emphasised by the Church because that was how you proved heretics to be wrong.

The many faults of argument have been listed in this book. The major fault is the lack of any constructive energy. Where do better ideas come from? How can you design a way forward for both sides?

Argument has its place but it is a very primitive and inefficient way of exploring a subject.

The Six Hats method of parallel thinking is a very powerful alternative to argument when you really want to explore a subject – rather than prove a point. It is now widely used, from top executives to four-year-olds in school. It reduces meeting times to a quarter or even a tenth of their normal length. The subject is thoroughly explored. There is now a lot of experience with the method. It has even started to be used by juries in court.

DEMOCRACY

The relevance of democracy to thinking is its perceived basis in attack and adversarial thinking. The emphasis both during and after elections is on 'destruction' not 'construction'. A government that does nothing is less easily attacked than one that is active.

Being clever in attack does not mean that you could suggest something better. So where is progress to come from?

It is possible that, in time, democracy will evolve into a more constructive mode.

COURTS OF LAW

Argument is central to the process of law. Being clever in argument may even seem to be more important than the validity of the case.

There are times when argument is the appropriate mode, but at other times there is room for design. There is a tendency that way with ADR (Alternative Dispute Resolution) and family court mediation.

The traditional view of law courts is that one side is right and the other is wrong. In some cases this is far from reality. There may be some right and some fault on both sides, especially in civil cases.

There is a need for a formal court of design to design the way forward for both parties.

THE MEDIA

The media in general and the press in particular have an ingrained negative and critical habit of mind. There are at least two possible explanations for this.

The first is that the press sees itself as the conscience and guardian of society. It sees its role as preventing tyranny, abuses and nonsenses being foisted on the public.

The second reason is that the negative mode is very much easier to operate than the positive mode. Many journalists and editors simply seem incapable of operating the positive mode. There is also the belief that the public are more interested in the negative than the positive.

The media and the press should take a lead in developing better thinking habits.

KNOWLEDGE AND INFORMATION

This is another very important point.

The belief is that all you need is knowledge and then you can do anything. The academic world has been concerned with description and understanding. If you can understand something then you will know what to do about it.

This is the 'road map' approach. You get a better and better road map. You fill in details and side roads. Once you have such a map, it is assumed you can get to wherever you want. All you need is a good road map – even if you have not learned to drive!

Schools and universities are all about knowledge. They always have been.

Computers have made it easier and easier to communicate and to store knowledge. The huge ability of computers to handle information means that the emphasis on information is getting even stronger. Marvellous search engines, such as Google and Yahoo!, mean that, for the first time in history, people can get direct and specific access to the information they need.

There is a downside to this. People start to believe that you do not have to think. We are coming to believe that the accumulation and analysis of knowledge will do all our practical thinking for us. All you need to do is to search on your computer and you will find the answer you need. I have found this to be the case with major corporations around the world. This lessens the thinking work for individuals and also removes all risk of being wrong – because the figures said so.

Information is essential, and there is no way that I would seek to diminish the key role of information. It is excellent, but not enough. We do need thinking as well.

We need thinking to look at the information in different ways. We need thinking to extract value from the information. We need thinking to put the information together in order to design the way forward.

If a fraction of the effort put into information was applied to thinking, the world would be a very different place.

UNIVERSITIES

Universities are obsessed with scholarship. This is hardly surprising. Universities were originally set up to make the wisdom of the past available to the world of today. That was a very important function. Universities have continued in exactly the same mode even though access to information has changed dramatically in a digital age. Where universities have been concerned with thinking, it is of the traditional type: analysis and debate. This is not good enough. There also needs to be a faculty of thinking.

Bright and eager minds go to university to learn about thinking. They end up with the word games of philosophy and not much about practical operational thinking.

We have paid very little attention to operational thinking. How do you make a practical choice? How do you design a strategy? How do you create new ideas? How do you negotiate?

In my work I have been concerned with the operational side of thinking – with creating ideas, with exploring a subject, with improving perception, etc.

The role of universities needs to shift dramatically from being a provider of information to being a developer of skills. These would include, among others, information access skills and thinking skills.

COMPUTERS

The role of computers in making information available has been mentioned above. This is excellent as long as it does not give the impression that enough information makes thinking unnecessary.

There is another danger. Information is fed into computers, which then analyse the information. Within corporations this information can determine decisions and set strategies. This is very dangerous, because you remain locked in the old concepts and perceptions. There is a real need to look at information in different ways.

Will computers ever learn to think? I believe so. We shall have to allow computers to do their own perceiving, because if we feed them our packaged perceptions they cannot really think. We may also have to move away from our 'digital' programming to 'field effect' programming, which more closely resembles the behaviour of the human brain.

THE RIGHT ANSWER

Add up the following numbers: 246, 918, 492, 501.

This is a simple addition. There is one, and only one, right answer: 2,157.

School and education are all about the right answer. What is the date of the battle of Waterloo? What is the capital of Mongolia? What is the population of Nigeria?

In all cases there is a right answer and you are supposed to know the right answer.

Is this bad? No, it is excellent. We need to know the right answers and the right way to do things. The result, however, is that there is very little room for creativity and for possibilities. We need to do more in these areas.

Increased chances

If you sit down to add up a column of numbers, or get your computer to do it for you, you know that, at the end of your effort, there will be a definite correct and useful answer. If you set out to manufacture an object you know that at the end of the manufacturing process you will have the completed object.

With creativity you do not have that certainty of output. You may have a focus and then make a creative effort (even using a lateral thinking tool) but the outcome cannot be guaranteed. You may have no ideas at all. You may have a few rather feeble ideas. As your skill improves, you will get more and better ideas but there is no guarantee.

Experiments have shown that groups using deliberate lateral thinking tools generate between 10 and 20 times as many ideas as those not using such tools. This is not surprising. Even so, there is no guarantee of a great idea.

If you go fishing, you cannot be sure that you are going to catch anything. Certainly you may have much more chance of catching a fish than someone who does not go fishing – but you cannot guarantee this on every occasion.

There is a need to shift the 'fishing' mind set. If you make a deliberate creative effort, you have an increased chance of having new ideas than if you make no such effort.

There is also a disinclination to have new ideas because a new idea means disruption, risk, hassle and bother. It seems better to continue with the existing routine until forced to change by circumstances or competitors.

To overcome this reluctance, it is necessary to make the acceptance, trial and use of new ideas easier. It should also be remembered that one of the main uses for creativity is to simplify operations. This is of direct benefit to those carrying out the operation.

It is always worth investing in creativity even if the outcome cannot be guaranteed. There is the increased chance that it will be. The benefits of new ideas can be huge. All that is required is some deliberate creative effort.

SCHOOLS AND EXAMS

Schools are all about information. Nothing else would fill the time allocated to education. This is grand baby-sitting with a more prestigious title.

We do need some of this information, but by no means all of it.

We are very happy with our thinking habits. We look at our scientific achievements and feel proud. This information is excellent – but it is not enough.

Education is a self-satisfying system. Schools teach what they want and then set their own examinations to assess how well the students have learned the material. There is no assessment as to whether what has been taught traditionally has any relevance in the modern world. There is no assessment of very important things (like thinking) that are not being taught.

Research by the Atkey organisation has shown that teaching my thinking as a separate subject improves performance in every other subject by between 30 and 100 per cent. There are thousands of schools around the world now doing this.

Far too little time is spent directly and deliberately on teaching thinking. Encouraging the asking of questions, helping with analysis and setting up debates are good but only teach one aspect of thinking. Thinking can be taught directly and deliberately as a skill and not just as a way of teaching another subject.

ART

Art plays an important role in developing perceptions and insights. People are encouraged to look at things in different ways and to see what they may not have seen before.

The down side of art is that it sometimes gives the impression that real life is all about emotions, feelings and, usually, anguish and negativity. These are, indeed, an important part of life – but only because we have never emphasised other aspects.

Art could do much more to encourage thinking.

LEADERSHIP

With the exception of a few countries, such as Venezuela, Malaysia and Singapore, leaders have been very negligent in encouraging thinking. This may be partly because they do not know what to do. It may also be due to their traditional advisers, who reject any new ideas.

With regards to education, the population is very badly served by its elected leaders. These leaders should be investigating what can be done to teach thinking. In my experience, they have shown no interest in doing so. As a result, students and others are deprived of the opportunity to develop their thinking skills.

There is also leadership at another level. World bodies like the UN need much better thinking. By definition, representative bodies are not going to be very good at thinking because they can only represent the traditional thinking of their own country. I did try for a while to set up a New Thinking Group at the UN but it was like dancing in treacle. I have instead set up a World Centre for New Thinking and a World Council for New Thinking (which includes several Nobel laureates). These bodies have been relatively inactive so far – but that will change.

CONTINUITY

This is another of the key points. People teaching in teacher training colleges want to teach what they themselves have been taught. The examination systems have a strong continuity and dictate what should be taught. There are so many strands of continuity in education that change is very difficult and depends on individual teachers and school principals. To be fair, part of this neglect is caused by innocence and ignorance. Many people simply do not know that thinking can be taught directly and deliberately as a skill. They do not know that there are formal techniques of idea creativity and new frameworks for exploring subjects. All they may know may come from a possibly one-sided piece written in one of the newspapers. Parents should be much more vigorous and vocal in demanding that things should happen. On behalf of their children, they are the 'consumers' of education, and consumers need to have a voice.

RIGHT/WRONG

In one of my books I invented the term 'proto-truth'. This describes something we hold to be true – providing we are trying to change it. This can be seen as applying to all truths or only some of them. It is the 'absolute' nature of truth that locks us into arrogance and complacency and prevents us doing any further thinking. There is no greater block to creativity than the belief that we already have the true answer.

In the same way we dismiss something that is obviously wrong. What could we get from something that is wrong? When we learn the mental operation of 'movement', then we can use this instead of judgement. From wrong ideas used as formal provocations we can get very useful ideas. The crazy suggestion that aeroplanes should land upside down leads to an interesting idea for supplying planes with a means of generating instant lift.

So we have possibilities that can develop into useful ideas. We also have 'wrong ideas' that can be treated as provocation and used for their 'movement value'.

The sharp judgement of right and wrong locks us into the past and into our existing frameworks and concepts. We need to dissolve this need to split things into right and wrong and unblock our creativity.

SUMMARY: TWENTY-THREE REASONS

These are the 23 reasons why world thinking is so poor and some ideas of what needs to be done to change that. You can probably add some more reasons of your own.

They could all be summarised in the word 'complacency'. We are so smug and satisfied with our existing thinking that we cannot see how poorly it serves us in the area of human affairs, creativity and design. More and more argument will not produce better ideas.

There is a phrase that I have used repeatedly in this book. The phrase is: 'Excellent – but not enough.' We are blocked and blinded by excellence. Our logic is excellent; our obsession with information is excellent – but these are not enough.

Unfortunately, our traditional thinking system demands that you show something to be bad before you can ask for change. That is not always possible. Our existing thinking is not bad. It is merely seriously inadequate. There is no mystery about what can be done to add additional methods of thinking.

16 What Can I Do?

THE PALACE OF THINKING

Somewhere, somehow I am going to set up a magnificent Palace of Thinking. I may be able to do it from my own resources or may have to rely on a particular country or individual to make it happen.

I shall be looking for an iconic and impressive building to give 'thinking' the importance and dignity it merits. It is no use having a back office on the fifteenth floor of a skyscraper.

This ambition symbolises the substance and purpose of this book. We take our thinking for granted. We are far too complacent about our thinking methods, which are in fact very limited. I have designed some additional software for thinking (for example, lateral thinking, the Six Hats and Septines), but there is much more to do.

The purpose of the Palace is to symbolise the importance of human thinking. It is also to emphasise the points I have made throughout this book: existing institutions are not interested in developing human thinking further because they are too satisfied with what we have now got. We need an institution that does.

The Palace will be a place for meetings. From time to time announcements will emanate from the Palace. There might even be a weekly report on 'World Thinking'.

It is precisely because there is no faculty or categorisation of 'thinking' that something like the Palace is needed to indicate that thinking is a skill that we should not take for granted.

The Palace of Thinking would have a number of functions:

1. To Generate Ideas

Periodic meetings would be held to focus on world issues and problems. Creative thinkers would be invited to participate in such meetings. The Palace would also have its own staff to generate ideas.

2. To Collect Ideas

To collect new ideas from any source. To act as a collection point for new ideas from any source. To ask for ideas from the public. The Internet will be a useful medium in this regard.

3. To Publish and Publicise New Ideas

The Palace would periodically publish new ideas. If the matter was urgent the ideas would be communicated via a press release to interested media. Interested media should ask to be on the distribution list for new ideas.

4. To Teach the Methods of Deliberate Creative Thinking

This is a secondary function of the Palace but will be available if there is sufficient demand for it.

5. To Symbolise the Importance of New Ideas

This may be the most important role for the Palace. To indicate that the analysis of information is not sufficient.

Youth

Someone once described to me the youth of today as being:

Sound-sodden sillies
Sports-sodden sillies
Sellebrity-sodden sillies (from celebrities used to sell)

While I do not agree with this, I can see the point. Youngsters are into distraction provided by the things listed.

Yet youth also wants achievement. The two things that matter to youngsters (and adults) are achievement and significance. Society has no method of providing youngsters with these possibilities. That is why some youngsters turn to crime: there is instant achievement and even a sense of importance (in a gang).

There are no easy remedies. The Boy Scouts at one time were a valuable initiative, but their appeal is no longer as wide as it should be. This is just one of the areas the Palace of Thinking would look into. Youngsters might be encouraged to use their minds instead of just watching and listening.

SUMMARY: WHAT CAN I DO?

The famous French philosopher René Descartes had a well-known saying: *Cogito, ergo sum.* This means 'I think, therefore I am'.

I have put together another saying: *Ago, ergo erigo.* This means 'I act, therefore I construct'.

The emphasis is on action not just on contemplation.

17   What Can You Do?

As I get older, my energy and resources become more limited. I do not mind carrying on a one-man crusade to improve the thinking of the world – but more will get done if more people want to get involved. I am most grateful to my trainers and others around the world who are teaching my thinking both in the business world and in schools.

But what can you do as a reader of this book?

INDIVIDUALS

You can let your friends know about this book. You can tell them about it. You can lend them your copy. You can buy a copy for them.

I am setting up a Society of Thinkers for those who wish to help in developing our thinking skills. Details can be found on the website: www.debonosociety.com.

As an individual you can write to politicians and ask

them what they are doing about the teaching of thinking in schools.

Some of my projects, like the Palace of Thinking, might need considerable resources, so those who are in a position to sponsor such projects may want to help. You may also want to let your own country know about the project to see if they would like to host the Palace.

PARENTS

You may want to make sure that your child is taught thinking at school. There are many children who are not good at the usual academic work at school but who are brilliant thinkers. If they get a chance to show this to themselves and to others, then their self-esteem rises and their overall performance improves.

Research has shown that teaching my thinking as a separate subject improves performance in every other subject by between 30 and 100 per cent. Should your child not have that advantage?

You should insist that your local school teaches thinking. You should write to the Minister of Education and ask what is being done about teaching thinking – and do not accept a vague general answer.

If all else fails, you can start to teach this thinking at home to your own children and even their friends. If the demand is sufficient I shall prepare a Home Thinking Kit.

EDUCATORS

Teachers, school principals and others who want to learn more about the teaching of thinking in education should contact people like Denise Inwood of the Atkey organisation, who has built up great experience in this area. There is also the de Bono Institute in Melbourne and the Edward de Bono Foundation in Ireland (and in the UK and Malta).

BUSINESS EXECUTIVES

There is a formal programme with certified instructors for teaching my thinking in business. Organisations that have used this programme include IBM, Siemens, Shell, Prudential and Citicorp, among others.

There are 1,300 certified instructors worldwide. You could make use of these instructors or arrange for in-house instructors to be trained within your own organisation.

It is also possible to become trained as an instructor yourself.

The instruction programme is headed by Kathy Myers at de Bono Thinking Systems in the USA. See page 251 for information.

FORMAL PROGRAMMES

There are the following formal programmes:

Education programmes

CoRT programme: This is a 60-lesson programme for schools. There are six parts and it is possible to use as many or as few of them as you like. The programme sets frameworks for perceptual thinking (PMI, OPV, C&S, and so on). CoRT 4 also includes lateral thinking tools.

Six Hats for Schools: This is the Six Hats exploratory framework as an alternative to argument.

Business programmes

These are not confined to business but can be used anywhere there is thinking to be done, such as in public service or community discussions.

Lateral Thinking: The specific lateral thinking tools for deliberate creativity.

Six Hats: A formal programme for teaching the use of the method for business meetings.

DATT: Direct Attention Thinking Tools. This provides tools for perceptual thinking and is equivalent to the CoRT programme in schools.

Simplicity: Methods and frameworks for simplifying existing operations. This is of particular importance for public service administration and similar organisations.

Six Value Medals: This programme deals with different types of value: Gold Medal for human values; Silver Medal for organisational values; Steel Medal for quality values; Glass Medal for innovation values; Wood Medal for ecology values; Brass Medal for perceptual values. There are also methods for carrying out value scans.

18 What Can Society Do?

The most important and fundamental point is to distinguish between 'idea creativity' and 'artistic creativity'. Unless that distinction is clearly made, there is no hope at all for progress. Governments and educational institutes will claim that they are already doing a great deal for 'creativity'. This is often true in the case of 'artistic creativity', but totally false in the case of idea creativity.

Doing a lot for artistic creativity does not mean doing anything at all for idea creativity. That is the situation at the moment.

We can look at four aspects of society to see how idea creativity could contribute in each area:

- Education
- Government
- Business
- Home

CREATIVITY AND EDUCATION

Here we encounter the very real problem caused by the failure of language to distinguish between idea creativity and artistic creativity. Schools claim that they are indeed doing a lot about creativity but this consists of some music, dancing, singing, painting and theatrical performances. They are doing nothing at all about idea creativity.

What can be done?

Pre-school

In the pre-school years and into primary school the ideal medium for creativity is drawing. A youngster can express in a drawing concepts he or she could never have described in words. I have had very young children draw complex negative feedback systems.

In a drawing you can see what is happening and you can ask questions: 'How does this happen?' You point to part of the drawing.

As mentioned earlier, through an education magazine I once set a series of design tasks for youngsters aged five years and upwards. The results are in two books: *The Dog Exercising Machine* and *Children Solve Problems*. The first book is full of designs for a machine to exercise dogs. The second book has a variety of design tasks, such as building a house more quickly, etc.

The designs of the youngsters are full of concepts. Sometimes the concepts are carried out in simple and crude ways.

Drawing is a very powerful way of getting young children to be creative, constructive and design-orientated. Note that these drawings are not the usual 'artistic' drawings of cottages with hollyhocks or flowers, etc. They are functional drawings showing some process or action.

Youngsters can also be encouraged to use the Six Hats framework, which they can handle from about the age of four onwards.

Primary school

Teaching my thinking as a separate subject has very powerful effects. The Atkey organisation showed improvement in every subject area of between 30 and 100 per cent. It is very important that the 'thinking' be taught as a separate subject labelled 'thinking'. This is because youngsters who are not good at the academic subjects often find they are very good at thinking. This increases their self-confidence tremendously. It also surprises the teachers.

The thinking taught is mainly the CoRT (Cognitive Research Trust) lessons. These are to do mainly with perceptual thinking and changes in perception. They also include some creativity. Perception, which is such a key element in thinking, is otherwise neglected in the curriculum.

As mentioned earlier, in Venezuela teaching this thinking is mandatory in all schools. There is widespread use in Australia, Canada, Singapore and Malaysia. There is growing use in India and China. In the United States and United Kingdom the use is patchy and depends on the energies of a school principal. Good research work has been done in the University of Verona in Italy by Michele de Bene, who showed powerful effects of teaching thinking directly.

Projects in primary school can also involve constructive, creative and design thinking. It is possible to set up a whole number of projects using newspaper, scissors and some glue. I once set youngsters the project of constructing a tower as high as possible from a single sheet of newspaper. The tower had to be stable and stand on its own. Several design concepts were used.

Secondary school

The general idiom of education is knowledge and analysis – the 'road map approach'.

This aspect of education is essential and very useful. But so is the creative, constructive and design aspect, which is totally neglected. It should be easy to cut down on some of the knowledge subjects (such as history) to devote time to thinking skills.

The drawing projects mentioned for primary school can also be used in secondary schools.

The CoRT thinking lessons are also used extensively in secondary schools. They provide tools and frameworks for improving perception. Logic without perception is more than useless – it is dangerous.

Hobbies are useful, but only some of them encourage creative and design thinking.

Achievement is very important to youngsters. Many of them drift into crime because this is the only place you can get a sense of short-term achievement. There is real need to develop other areas of constructive achievement for youngsters.

University

Two years ago I was giving a lecture at the World University Presidents' Summit in Bangkok. There were about 2,000 university presidents at the meeting.

I pointed out that universities were out of date. The origin of universities was to bring the wisdom and knowledge of the past and make it available to the students of today. In a digital age, it is possible to get all the knowledge you need without a university.

So universities should be teaching skills:

- Information skills and how to obtain and assess information.
- Thinking skills including creative, design, constructive and perceptual thinking (not just analysis and logic).
- People skills. How to deal with and manage people.
- Operational skills. Designing and carrying out projects.

There are other skills that could be added to this list.

Universities could also be more involved with society, for example, by organising forums to discuss specific issues. They could also organise creative approaches to different social issues.

It is no longer enough for universities to be 'little closed houses of knowledge'.

CREATIVITY AND GOVERNMENT

As mentioned earlier, democracy is considered the best system of government, but that does not mean that it is good. The adversarial system of parliament does not encourage creative thinking and new ideas. So half the elected talent is lost.

I had a discussion with the Prime Minister of Mauritius, who is a reader of my books. I suggested that every Monday parliament should use the Six Hats method. The speaker would announce 'Yellow Hat Time' and members would only speak if they had something to say. I suspect that party discipline would mean that no one would offer any positive views on an idea proposed by the other party.

There could be a special committee formed by members from both parties. This committee could only be positive and offer new ideas. It would never be the role of this committee to attack. This National Council for New Ideas would be a formal challenge for potential new ideas.

Governments should have a Minister for New Ideas who would look after new ideas in every field. A Minister for Innovation is a step in the right direction, but somewhat weaker. It is the difference between waiting for new ideas and making them happen.

Information and ideas

There is the persisting belief that information is enough. Governments have think tanks that collect and analyse information. It is assumed that this will produce new ideas. But the analysis of information is not enough, because the information can be perceived through the old concepts. There is a real need for a formal and deliberate effort to create new ideas. New ideas do not just evolve over time. They need to be created.

Creativity and the UN

Many years ago I tried to set up a Creative Thinking Group within the UN. There were various meetings and Kofi Annan, before he became Secretary General, was at one of them.

There was an appreciation of the real need for new ideas in conflict situations and elsewhere. At the same time there was the underlying feeling that representatives of different countries were there to represent the thinking of those countries and not to create new ideas. A new idea might be contrary to the policy of a particular country. A representative might even generate a new idea that was contrary to the position of his or her country.

In short, the UN did not exist to do its own thinking, but to represent the thinking of the member nations.

Where from?

New ideas are a mathematical necessity. Information is not enough.

Applying judgement to conflict situations is not enough. There is a real need to 'design a way forwards'.

Problems such as poverty, food prices and AIDS may need some additional thinking. This is not to imply that existing thinking is inadequate, but that new ideas can open up new possibilities that may need to be considered. But where are these ideas to come from?

The UN is not designed to put forward such new ideas. If an individual country puts forward a new idea, it will be seen as an extension of the policy of that particular country. Even if the idea is indeed excellent, it will be regarded with suspicion and resentment. The US can produce many good ideas but they are too easily regarded as an exercise in US imperialism.

There is a need for a neutral, independent body that can generate, collect and publicise new ideas and new possibilities. Once these become public, they can be considered. They might be ignored or they might be used. They might influence current thinking. In all cases, it is better to have some new ideas rather than none at all.

CREATIVITY AND BUSINESS

What can be done to increase creativity in a business organisation?

Take it seriously

The most important thing about creativity is to take it seriously.

Why do we not take creativity seriously when we know that much of progress depends on creativity?

The first reason is that we do not understand creativity. This has always been a mystery. We can see the results but do not know how it happened. By the time you have read this book you will know how idea creativity works.

The second reason is that we do not know what to do about it. We assume that ideas just happen from time to time and there is nothing you can do about it. You can also borrow, copy or steal ideas from others. Most people do not realise that you can use creativity formally and creatively. You can sit down and generate new ideas.

Corporations take finance very seriously. They take legal matters very seriously. They take research very seriously. They do not take creativity seriously at all.

As discussed below, in every organisation there is a need for a CCO or Chief Creativity Officer. That is a formal position. The person occupying that position should be senior but not so senior that he or she does not have time for it.

The CCO does not need to be personally creative but must appreciate creativity. If the CCO is personally creative, there is the danger of belittling the ideas of others. The CCO must be a good 'people person', a good communicator and full of energy. Other activities of the CCO, such as setting up a Centre for Creativity, will be described below.

It is not just a matter of finding and collecting creative people, however. Creativity is a skill that everyone can learn. There is a need for formal training since education has not provided this. Generating over 20,000 ideas in an afternoon is the result of the skilled use of a lateral thinking technique – not of talent.

Creativity greatly enhances the existing assets and potential of any organisation, not just businesses. It is not enough just to wait for it to happen. You need to take creativity seriously and to take action.

All governments should have a Minister for New Ideas or, at least, a Minister for Innovation. The word 'innovation' means putting into action an idea that is new for that organisation. Creativity means the generation of an original idea. Innovation has its value but is weaker than creativity.

Exhortation

This is much used but is not very effective. Urging people to be creative is part of the general 'lip service' that is paid to creativity because people do not know what else to do.

Expectation

This is essential and is much more powerful. The chief executive, and others, need to make very clear that people are expected to put forward new ideas. Executives and others are very good at sensing the game they are supposed to be playing. The usual game is 'continuity and problem solving'. This means to continue to do what you are supposed to do and to solve problems that arise. New ideas are not seen as part of the game and may even be seen as hassle and bother to everyone around. So it needs to be made clear, in a concrete way, that new ideas are part of the job specification.

Time and meetings

This means specific meetings with creativity as the direct focus. The subject of the meeting is announced in advance. During the meetings the lateral thinking tools are used. Such meetings should be frequent but not too frequent. They should not last too long. If meetings are perceived as lasting too long, people will find excuses not to attend. Ninety minutes is ample. Time can also be set aside for individual creative thinking. There is a bank where senior executives set aside between 9am and 9.30am for individual creative thinking. No meetings are called during this time. Secretaries do not put through calls. Most thinking during the day is about urgent matters that need to be attended to. Important matters that could benefit from new thinking do not get this thinking. So setting aside time specifically for this purpose is well worthwhile. It is important to be consistent and rigid about such procedures or they fall apart.

Chief Creativity Officer (CCO)

We cannot use the term Chief Ideas Officer because CIO is already taken by Chief Information Officer. Creativity needs to be treated as seriously as information, legal matters, finance, etc. The CCO should be senior enough to have access to the highest levels in the organisation but not so senior that he or she does not have time for the job. The CCO needs to be a people person who is good at communicating, organising and encouraging people. He or she does not have to be especially creative. In fact, it may be better if the person is not too creative, because the ideas of others can then be treated more neutrally. The CCO organises training, sets up the Creative Hit List (described in Chapter 2) and may set up a Creativity Centre.

The Creativity Centre

People are not motivated to have ideas if no one is going to listen to their new idea. People around you, and your immediate superiors, often do not welcome the disruption of a new idea about which they might be expected to do something. The Creativity Centre is there as a forum and listening place for new ideas. The Centre can also act as the organising point for the activities of the CCO.

David Tanner came to a seminar I gave in Toronto many years ago. He invited me to DuPont, where I gave several seminars to senior management. He became, in effect, the CCO. He set up a Creativity Centre. He also set up a network of creative people who could communicate with each other. There were many other practical innovations he made in this field. Based on his experience of organising creativity in a large organisation, he is now working as a consultant and has written several books about his experience.

Publication

Although most creative people would not admit it, creative people like other people to know about their new ideas. Even if the idea cannot be acted upon, they would like the idea to be publicised. This is understandable. So it is important in an organisation to have some way of making ideas visible. This can mean a specific 'creative newsletter' or it can be part of the usual internal newsletter. Nothing is more motivating to a creative person.

Networks

As mentioned above, there is value in putting creatively motivated people in touch with each other through a network (as David Tanner did in DuPont). They can exchange ideas, set up meetings, define tasks, help each other, etc. The danger of a network of enthusiastic people is that others might feel excluded and feel that creativity is not for them, but only for the special people in the network. So networks should not be too tightly configured.

Department

If creativity is so important, it might seem logical to have a special department of creatively motivated people who would do all the creative thinking needed. This would be equivalent to the normal research department. The real danger here, as with networks, is that other people feel excluded and feel that creativity is only for that department. Since ideas are needed everywhere and from everyone, this is a real danger. It is probably better, in business organisations, not to have such a specific department, but to have a strong Creativity Centre that can fulfil the organising functions of a department but is open-ended and not restricted to a small group of people.

Celebration

New ideas should be celebrated. This involves the publication mentioned earlier but can also mean special gestures of appreciation, such as a Creativity Medal or other award for new ideas. Such celebrations not only motivate the people who have had the ideas but indicate that new ideas are expected and appreciated. This is very different from having to persuade someone to listen to a new idea, which is usually the case.

Training

Many businesses have had their people formally trained in lateral thinking (DuPont, IBM, Prudential, Siemens, etc.) Many now have internal trainers who can carry on the training internally.

Motivation

In my experience, the interest in creativity has usually been driven by the CEO, who knows that creativity is needed. This sets the mood and motivation for the organisation. Expectation is very important. If people know that they are expected to have ideas, they will have ideas. If they believe that their job is 'continuity and problem solving', they will find new ideas too much bother.

One bank told me they used to have a few suggestions every month from their staff. After training in lateral thinking they now have over 600 a month.

Motivation and skill go together and they build on each other. Success in creativity increases the motivation, which increases the skill.

CREATIVITY AND THE HOME

Youngsters often take home from school the thinking lessons they have learned. These may be the Six Hats method, or the CoRT perceptual tools. They introduce these tools to their parents – who then use them.

The ideas that I have mentioned for the pre-school age all work well at home. These include setting drawing tasks and then discussing together the output.

Parents can set thinking games for children and play these games with the children. For example, a parent might say 'Suppose all cars had to be painted yellow. Do a PMI on that.' The PMI is a CoRT tool and stands for Plus, Minus and Interesting.

Parents can set aside one evening a week as a 'thinking evening'. Friends' and neighbours' children can be invited to take part. Youngsters really enjoy thinking, as an idea is an achievement.

In discussions, and even in quarrels, the Six Hats framework can be used to explore the situation fully.

With older children, specific creative tasks can be set and then the lateral thinking tools can be used to generate new ideas.

In the future I shall be writing more fully about 'Family Thinking Sessions'. If the school is not going to teach thinking, then you can do it at home. If the school is teaching thinking, you can still teach it at home too. Thinking is a life skill.

19 Values

The purpose of thinking is to allow us to enjoy and to deliver our values.

Thinking without values is meaningless and achieves nothing.

Values without thinking have been responsible for persecutions and all manner of nastiness. If someone has different values, then that person must be wrong.

Although values are so central to thinking, we have paid very little direct attention to values. We have assumed that everyone will recognise the values that matter to them.

TRUTH

We have always considered truth to be more important than value in thinking. Once again there was the influence of the Church in the Middle Ages. Truth was everything. And if you followed the 'true way', then values could come about of their own accord.

Just as discovery is to truth so design is to value. The purpose of design is to deliver the values we want.

Truth is very important – but so are values. Truth by itself is not enough.

Just as a scientific discovery has to be turned into a practical application (in medicine or the commercial world), so truth needs to be turned into value.

VAGUE

We have a very vague approach to values. We reckon that we know what we want or value and we know what we do not want.

A flock of birds is flying overhead. One person looks up and says: 'There are a lot of birds about today.'

Another person looks up and says: 'Do you see the goose over there? Then there is the kestrel. And that might be a magpie.'

The first person just sees birds and the second person has learned to recognise different birds. In the same way it is possible to learn to recognise different values in a very specific way.

Once we have learned to recognise values, we can also look for them specifically. We need a framework for distinguishing one value from another.

THE SIX VALUE MEDALS

In my book *The Six Value Medals,* I provide a framework for distinguishing one type of value from another. I have mentioned it earlier in this book but it is so important that it is worth repeating here.

In the book there are also methods of setting out a value scan. This is a visual display of values. Value scans from different people can then be compared. The points of difference are not obvious. They can be discussed. This is a much more precise process than arguing about values in a vague way.

Gold Medal: These are human values. They are values that apply specifically to human beings. There may be values like praise, achievement, pride and significance. There can also be negative values like humiliation and being ignored. The value medals include both positive and negative values.

Silver Medal: These are organisational values. For a business corporation it may be a matter of profits, market share or brand image. For a political organisation it may be public perception or votes. For the organisation of a family unit it may be cooperation, peace or honesty.

Steel Medal: These are quality values. Steel is supposed to have certain qualities, such as strength and durability. Quality values of any sort come under the Steel Medal.

The intrinsic nature of an item or procedure determines its purpose. Quality determines how well it fulfils that purpose. Is it what it is supposed to be? Does it do what it is supposed to do?

Glass Medal: Glass is a simple but very versatile material. With creativity you can make all sorts of things from glass. So the Glass Medal is about innovation and creativity. This medal looks at new ideas and new suggestions. It may even be that an idea has no value at the moment other than its newness. The Glass Medal allows us to look at and appreciate creative effort.

Wood Medal: This medal is to do with ecology and the surroundings. This is not limited to nature. If a factory is the major employer in a small town, then policy changes might have a strong effect on that town. That is ecology.

Brass Medal: These are 'perceived values'. They are extremely important but usually neglected. How will this decision be perceived? You may do something that is worthwhile but is perceived very badly. You may do something that is not so good but produces a positive perception. Brass looks like gold but is not. In the same way, perceived values may not relate to real values. Perceived values need to be considered directly. It is not enough to suppose that if you do something worthwhile it will be perceived positively.

SEARCH, RECOGNITION AND ASSESSMENT

Once we have a way of distinguishing different types of value, we can search for each of the different values in a situation. Some change is proposed. What would the effects be under each of the value medals? We can look at the consequences of the change through the frame of each value medal. What might be the positive values? What might be the negative values?

In assessing any situation we can now pick out and assess the different values (in the book, a method of giving a strength to values is provided). It is like the person who had learned to pick out the different birds in the flock flying overhead.

Once we can see a type of value clearly, we are able to assess its strength and importance. This is not possible if values are all mixed together and only seen in a vague sort of way as with the flock of birds.

WHY SIX?

Why six Value Medals and six Thinking Hats?

We know from psychology that the brain can perceive a maximum of seven things at any one time. If there are more than that, the brain starts to subdivide. So from the point of view of perception, seven would be the maximum useful number of categories.

I prefer to use six. That leaves one unused category should experience indicate that there is a real need for another category. It has not done this so far.

20 The Right to Think

As far as I know, and subject to correction, I believe that 'the right to think' is not spelled out in the UN Declaration of Human Rights.

There are several possible explanations for this. There is no specific right to walk, to talk, to eat or to breathe. So it is assumed that thinking is a natural function and there is no need to spell out any specific right to do so. This is a very bad mistake. At a primitive, animal level, there is some natural thinking, but that is very simple and crude. It consists mainly of recognising situations and applying the right routine.

Another possible explanation is that it is assumed that thinking comes naturally under the heading of 'education'. This is another bad mistake. The thinking taught in education, at best, is about judgement, analysis and debate. This is only a small part of thinking. To be sure, there are some schools and even countries where thinking is now taught explicitly, but they are few.

INSTRUCTION

You might have the right to play tennis or to play the piano, but unless someone teaches you how to do it, that right is meaningless. Everyone knows that children need to be taught how to read and write. It would never be enough to say, 'You have the right to read and write – now get on with it!'

Of course, it will be argued that if 'instruction in thinking' is mentioned, then totalitarian regimes will instruct youngsters how to think according to the rules of that regime. This is not to be encouraged. Yet we have to realise that all religions have done this since their inception.

It is no more difficult to teach thinking in a neutral manner than it is to teach mathematics. Around the world there are various regimes of different political natures that are happily teaching my thinking in their schools. This is the case in Christian countries, Islamic countries, Buddhist countries and in the old days of Communist countries. Thinking is a skill, like mathematics, and is not political.

PERMISSION TO THINK

In the Republic of Ireland, Jim O'Sullivan decided to teach my thinking to his employees at an electronics company. They saved so much money that he could afford to pay them more. At one point some people from the shop floor designed a new computer keyboard in which they subsequently invested $5 million – and it was a sales success.

I have told elsewhere the story of the Argentinian who ran a textile company. He gave his staff 'permission to think' and instruction on how to do it. At that time the company was half the size of its nearest competitor. Today, a few years later, the company is 10 times the size of that competitor.

There is a huge human resource potential in employees if they are given permission to think – and some simple instruction on how to do it.

ABSURD

It is an absurd and antique attitude to believe that thinking is natural and therefore needs no instruction.

It is an absurd and antique attitude to believe that normal education teaches sufficient thinking.

There is a real need to teach thinking deliberately and directly as a separate subject in education (both schools and universities). This means thinking in its fullest sense, not just logic and argument. Judgement is an essential part of thinking, just as the rear left wheel is an essential part of a motor car – but it is not sufficient: excellent, but not enough!

How is it that we have progressed so far without this realisation?

Epilogue

I want to repeat, yet again, that I have no quarrel with our existing thinking systems. They are excellent and do their work very well.

'Excellent but not enough' has been the theme of this book.

We need to supplement our existing thinking methods with some additional thinking software.

We need a method for formal creative thinking: that is the lateral thinking methods.

We need a method for exploring a subject when argument is inefficient and inappropriate: that is the Six Hats method.

We need to pay a great deal more attention to perceptual thinking: that is the CoRT programme and the DATT programme.

We need to look at values more directly: that is the Six Value Medals programme.

There is also a book of mine about the Six Action Shoes

that seeks to clarify different types of action. I have not covered this method in this book.

There is also the new method of the Septine.

All these provide additional software for areas and uses that are not adequately covered by existing thinking software.

With computers, software is designed for a purpose – so is it with these additional methods.

No amount of logical searching for the truth will produce a new idea.

Our existing thinking is simply not good enough. While we are rightly concerned with the environment and with problem areas, we are far too complacent about our thinking – which is by far the most important of all areas.

De Bono Thinking Systems

There is a network of over 1,000 instructors and trainers worldwide who are accredited to the de Bono Thinking Systems. They have considerable experience in teaching my thinking to corporations. Thousands have been trained in this way around the world. Please contact www.debonothinkingsystems.com to be put in touch with the distributor in the country of your choice.

Should you wish to contact me directly regarding seminars and talks, the best way is through my assistant at: paddyhills@hotmail.com

I am also setting up a club for individuals who are genuinely interested in the important matter of human thinking. This new club can be accessed through: www.debonosociety.com

The de Bono Thinking Systems network can provide training in: Lateral Thinking; Six Hats; Six Value Medals; Simplicity; Focus on Facilitation; and DATT (Direct Attention Thinking Tools).

For information on the Thinking Curriculum that is used in schools, contact me directly at: edwdebono@msn.com

For information on the teaching of thinking as a subject in schools, please contact Denise Inwood through: www.blueskyskills.co.uk

The Edward de Bono Foundation

The Edward de Bono Foundation is concerned with the teaching of constructive thinking in Education and Management. For further information contact:

The Edward de Bono Foundation
PO Box 2397
Dunshaughlin Business Park
Dunshaughlin
Co Meath
Ireland

Tel: +353 1 8250466
Fax: +353 1 8250467

Email: debono@iol.ie

Website: www.edwarddebonofoundation.com

Index

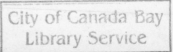

The Six Value Medals

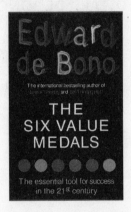

Whether as an individual, a business executive or a director you are looking to be the best, this is the book that could improve your company, your career – and your life.

Values are central to everything: the purpose of any business or government organisation is to deliver value, and increasingly we seek this in our personal lives as well. Yet values are vague and intangible. In this groundbreaking book, Edward de Bono reveals an exciting but simple framework for individuals and business leaders alike for making creative, effective decisions, based on embracing key values – the focus of the 21st century.

Offering sound advice on decision making and better thinking practice, *The Six Value Medals* thwarts traditional thinking habits, demonstrates how you can deal with values in a much more definite way and enables you to highlight your strengths while pinpointing areas for improvement, helping you and your company become more successful.

It's time to start using the Six Value Medals!

9780091894597   £8.99

www.rbooks.co.uk

How to Have Creative Ideas

In *How to Have Creative Ideas*, Edward de Bono outlines 62 different games and exercises, using random words as a provocation to encourage creativity and lateral thinking.

Simple, practical and fun, this book is for anyone who wants to have great ideas.

9780091910488   £8.99

www.rbooks.co.uk

Six Frames for Thinking about Information

In a world saturated with facts and figures as never before, how do we focus our attention to make the most of information at our fingertips?

Using his 'Six Frames' technique, Edward de Bono shows us how to direct our attention in a conscious manner, rather than always letting it get pulled to the unusual and irrelevant. Just as we can decide to look north, west or even south-east, so we can set up a framework for directing our attention and, like all of de Bono's techniques, it is simple, effective and will utterly change the way you interpret information.

9780091924195

£8.99

www.rbooks.co.uk

H+ (Plus) A New Religion?

Edward de Bono has revolutionised the way we think. And now he's about to change the way we live our lives . . .

In this groundbreaking, thought-provoking book, Edward de Bono offers us a new way of living based on an entirely positive way of life. In H+ (Plus) he provides a framework for happiness through daily acts of help or contribution. Whether this is offering other people something to laugh at or helping an elderly person cross the road, these altruistic acts lead to a sense of achievement, and from achievement comes self-esteem and a belief in oneself.

Discover the secret to leading a fuller, happier, healthier, more positive way of life.

9780091910471   **£6.99**

www.rbooks.co.uk